Christmas wi
Mand

An eyewitness account of South Africa's first years of democracy

Adrian Hadland

Low Battery Books

First published in Low Battery Books in 2025

Cover designed by Lizbe Coetzee

ISBN: 9781068337031

For more information and access to other titles: adrian.hadland.com

DEDICATION

This one is for my mum who has been a tower of strength and support for as long as I can remember.

Abbreviations

ANC - African National Congress
APLA - Azanian People's Liberation Army
AZAPO - Azanian People's Organisation
CODESA - Convention for a Democratic South Africa
COSATU - Congress of South African Trade Unions
CP - Conservative Party
DP - Democratic Party
EU - European Union
GNU – Government of National Unity
IEC - Independent Electoral Commission
IFP - Inkatha Freedom Party
MDC - Movement for Democratic Change (of Zimbabwe)
MSA - Muslim Students' Association
NCTU – National Council of Trade Unions
NEC - National Executive Committee (of the ANC)
NP - National Party
NNP - New National Party
PAC - Pan Africanist Congress
PAGAD - People Against Gangsterism and Drugs
PRC - People's Republic of China
RDP - Reconstruction and Development Programme
SADF - South African Defence Force
SCOPA - Standing Committee on Public Accounts
TEC - Transitional Executive Committee
TRC - Truth and Reconciliation Commission
TREWITS - Counter Revolutionary Target Information Centre (Afrikaans acronym)
UCT - University of Cape Town
UN - United Nations
UDM - United Democratic Movement
WTO - World Trade Organisation
ZANU-PF - Zimbabwe African National Union – Patriotic Front

South Africa Timeline 1989-2004

1989 - FW de Klerk replaces PW Botha as president. The young, pragmatic, and *verligte* (enlightened) De Klerk realises the current form of apartheid is a "cul-de-sac". De Klerk meets Mandela, starting the process of reconciliation. Many African National Congress (ANC) activists are freed and public facilities desegregated.

1990 - ANC unbanned. Mandela released from Victor Venter Prison. An agreement called the *Pretoria Minute* suspended the armed struggle of the ANC, bringing the State of Emergency to an end.

1990 – Tripartite Alliance (or "Revolutionary Alliance" or simply "The Alliance") formed between the ANC, Congress of South African Trade Unions (COSATU), and the SA Communist Party.

1991 - Start of multi-party talks at CODESA I (The Convention for a Democratic South Africa), the first plenary, to conceptualise the new constitution for the country. National peace accord signed on 14th September 1991.

1992 - Increased factional fighting between ANC and Inkatha Freedom Party (IFP) members leads to township battles. Boipatong massacre of 45 residents killed by Zulu hostel dwellers.

1992 - CODESA II, the second plenary, breaks down, as Mandela withdraws from negotiations. He accused the government of being complicit over the Boipatong massacre and instead recommended mass action.

1992 - ANC's "rolling mass action" met with tragedy at the Bisho massacre of 29 people. The Ciskei homeland army opened fire on protest marchers. A new urgency to find a settlement spurred the government, ANC, and IFP to resume negotiations.

1992 - Joe Slovo, former leader of the SACP, secured a major breakthrough in the negotiation process by presenting the "sunset clauses". A coalition government (ANC/NP/IFP) would lead the country for five years following the elections, while existing (white) civil servants would have guarantees of land, jobs, and security. Even today, the sunset clauses are controversial, and many accuse the ANC of "selling out" their Freedom Charter ideals.

1993 - South African Communist Party leader and Commander in Chief of MK Chris Hani assassinated on 10th April by Janusz Waluś. His assassination seen as a turning point in the country's transition - Mandela addresses the nation, speaking like a president, and the negotiation process galvanises into action. The election date is decided for 27th April 1994.

1993 - AWB crashes a "Viper" armoured vehicle through the doors of the World Trade Centre in Kempton Park on 25th June, where the negotiations were being held. AWB members took control of the building briefly but departed peacefully. White right-wing groups vehemently opposed the negotiation process as they felt their interests were not being considered.

1993 - Agreement on interim constitution of the country occurred in the early hours of 18th November.

1994 - Bophuthatswana crisis unfolds as splinter white nationalists from the AWB invades homeland on 11th March. High profile killing of AWB militants threaten to destabilise peace process. Images of the dying AWB commanders, taken by Kevin Carter and Greg Marinovich, spread globally and draw the news spotlight to Southern Africa.

1994 - Township battles, the bombing campaign by the white-right, and IFP attacks precluded the 1994 election. Upwards of 20,000 IFP members stormed Shell House (ANC headquarters in Johannesburg) on 28th March where ANC officials opened fire, killing 19 people. Bomb explodes in Bree Street, Johannesburg on 25th April, killing nine people. Bomb explodes at Jan Smuts International Airport on 28th April, killing 21 people.

1994 - First all-race elections in the country over three days in April. ANC wins by landslide. Mandela becomes first democratic president and leads the Government of National Unity between National Party, ANC, and IFP.

1994 - Final sanctions on South Africa are lifted and the country resumes its seat in UN General Assembly. Township battles calm, the nation breathes a cautious sign of relief.

1996 - Truth and Reconciliation Commission (TRC) with Archbishop Desmond Tutu as chair begins hearings on human rights crimes committed by both government officials and liberation movements during apartheid.

1996 - Government adopts new constitution on 8th May and is promulgated by President Mandela on 18th December.

1996 - National Party withdraws from Government of National Unity on 9th May, leaving the ANC and IFP as sole members until the 1999 election, when the GNU lapsed.

1998 - TRC report brands apartheid a crime against humanity and finds ANC accountable for human rights abuses.

1998 - The government procures weaponry and military aircraft to modernise the defence force, under the Strategic Defence Acquisition. It became known simply as the Arms Deal and was plagued by allegations of corruption, implicating Jacob Zuma, Thabo Mbeki, politician Tony Yengeni, and businessman Schabir Shaik. Patricia de Lille acted as whistleblower in 1999 with numerous bribery allegations.

1999 - ANC wins second general elections. Thabo Mbeki becomes second democratic president.

1999 - on 28 October, Mbeki gives speech to the National Council of Provinces and questions whether the government should distribute anti-retroviral (ARV) drugs to combat AIDS. The epidemic was exploding in the country at the time.

2001 - Mbeki chairs the "Presidential Advisory Panel on AIDS" which debated the significance of the HIV/AIDS link and need for AIDS testing in the country. Mbeki argues that alleviating poverty in the country is more important than relying on expensive Western medicine. Mbeki's approval rating plummets and he acknowledges he caused "confusion" by challenging the mainstream view of AIDS.

2002 - Bomb explodes in Soweto and Pretoria, thought to be the work of right-wing extremists. Police also charge 17 right-wingers with plotting against the state

2004 - ANC wins third general election. Mbeki retains a second term as president.

Source: Jones, B. (2021) *Elections and TV News in South Africa: Desperately Seeking Depth.* Basingstoke: Palgrave.

Preface

It is easy to forget how close South Africa came to catastrophe and civil war in the weeks before its first democratic election in 1994.

A right-wing bombing campaign killed more than 100 people in cities and towns across the country, including at the offices of the Independent Electoral Commission, organisers of the poll. "Nine killed as car bomb rocks Jo'burg", screamed one headline. "Bomb madness grips South Africa," yelled another.

Former military general General Constand Viljoen claims he was ready and able to mobilise 60,000 troops and a squadron of fighter jets to defend a white homeland, or *volkstaat*. One of the more than 200 right-wing extremist groups that had sprouted since the unbanning of the African National Congress broke into the state armoury in November 1993 and stole more than three tons of equipment, including 100,000 rounds of ammunition, 400 handgrenades and 200 mortars.

The Inkatha Freedom Party refused to join the electoral process and instead waged a prolonged and bloody conflict with the African National Congress, particularly but not only in KwaZulu-Natal.

The country was awash with weapons and belligerence, from the police and military organisations of the former apartheid homelands to the three major liberation armies who had confronted apartheid's soldiers and police officers for three decades.

South Africans began to hoard tinned foods, petrol and water in anticipation of the worst. Many who could afford to leave the country did so and watched on from somewhere safe.

Not only was South Africa a mess of violence and death, it teetered on the brink of self-destruction. Little wonder that the world held its breath in expectation of a bloody, racial conflagration.

When the election was eventually held in 1994 - surprisingly in relative peace -

Nelson Mandela became South Africa's first democratically-elected president.

I was one of a small group of journalists who had closely followed the twists and turns of what had been a very difficult, violent but fascinating road to freedom and power.

The story, as it unfolded, was remarkably complex. There was, of course, the huge legacy of 300 years of race-based rule, formalised as apartheid in the 1940s. And there was the pain and suffering that accompanied apartheid's imposition and enforcement. There was also an international dimension as the anti-apartheid movement and its allies worked hard to isolate South African economically, culturally and politically. Internally, ancient divisions and animosities bubbled and occasionally burst into the open.

Mandela was in power for only one term before handing the reins to his successor, Thabo Mbeki. Perhaps no world leader has ever faced an inheritance quite as poisonous or as troublesome. It wasn't like a few laws needed to be changed to set the country on the road to democracy. It was all laws, more than 500 during Mandela's only term as president.

A new Constitution was required. In addition, laws were introduced and passed when the law makers knew full well there was precious little chance of these same laws actually being enforced. But that was the choice Mandela and his ministers faced. Change the law and the Constitution and hope, in time, that these changes would grow roots and gradually evolve the landscape in the direction of what was intended.

This book tells the dramatic story of these extraordinary times from the vantage point of a front row seat in the new multiracial democratic Parliament. Here you will find many of the key personalities speaking from the heart about the rapid changes affecting their country.

You will hear both Inkatha leader Mangosuthu Buthelezi and deputy president FW De Klerk speak of the tension within the government of national unity established after the first democratic election in 1994. You will hear too from Mandela himself, from his successor Thabo Mbeki and from a range of other key contributors to South Africa's transition from the Pan Africanist Congress's Patricia de Lille and the first female, black Speaker of the National Assembly Dr Frene Ginwala to later president Cyril Ramaphosa and Joe Seremane from the Democratic Party.

In these pages you will read of the work of the Truth and Reconciliation Commission trying to untangle the web of violence and death in order to pave a way forward to peace but also of small rural communities wrestling with their legacy of division and oppression at the very moment they look forward to a future of democracy and hope.

It is all too clear, looking back at these accounts, how difficult the transition to democracy was and how fraught with challenges.

What struck me most during the almost 15 years that I covered South Africa's transition from apartheid to democracy was the extraordinary calibre of the people involved in negotiating and installing the country's democratic dispensation. People from all sides of the political spectrum showed remarkable tolerance, compassion and intelligence in agreeing to compromise, rework, change attitude or look afresh at issues and, in so doing, reach agreement on how things should go forward. This was the real miracle of the South African transition, the gathering of a generation of brilliant, empathetic and articulate leaders - led by Mandela - and their collective creation of a blueprint for a new, free country.

I don't claim that this collection of essays, articles and columns represents a comprehensive account of South Africa's journey to democracy. Key moments and key people are missing. But I hope it nonetheless presents an in-depth, insider's account of what happened and how. Not many other journalists sat near Mandela as he was inaugurated as president, watched as he addressed Parliament for the first time or was within touching distance during his divorce trial. Fewer still were blessed with his chatty phone calls or were invited to share Christmas lunch with him and his family at his home in Qunu.

During almost 15 years of political reporting in South and southern Africa, I have sat face to face with the leaders from a wide range of parties to hear their wishes and fears. Many speak frankly and honestly in this volume and I have tried to reflect their views fairly. Some show humility, others the scars of trauma and loss.

I hope everyone who reads this book will find some memory triggered or some insight into what this journey meant to the people who led the way and to those who were affected by what transpired. I hope you will delight in the joyful repartee and banter of South Africa's colourful elected representatives, will chuckle at the ironies and contradictions and will recall with interest and perhaps pride the steps on the way to accomplishing a journey that at times looked impossible.

This book contains an account of South Africa's emergence as a democracy that otherwise would have been lost. The transition to democracy took place in the mid to late 1990s, just as the internet was about to emerge and the digital world was taking root. Little of what you will read here has been saved. Independent Newspapers, owners of titles such as the *Cape Times* and the *Sunday Times*, destroyed their substantial Cape Town cuttings library in the early 2000s. Thousands of files were left in a big heap in a garage and eventually discarded. Much of the record of South Africa's politics at this crucial time has gone while the memory of those hope-filled days has been overwhelmed by new challenges and crises.

I managed to salvage an armful of files from the huge pile in the Argus garage and had fortunately kept many of the columns and articles I had written during this important time. As a parliamentary correspondent for *Business Day*, senior writer for *The Sunday Independent*, Political Editor of the *Cape Argus*, Southern African correspondent for Lisbon's daily paper, *Publico*, and correspondent for the wire service UPI, I found myself in close proximity to all that was happening, on and beneath the surface, during South Africa's transition. I interviewed leaders, attended court cases, committee meetings, press conferences, Truth Commission hearings and cocktail parties and watched from the press gallery as South Africa's new leadership attempted to shape a new country free of the violence and prejudice of the past. I wrote weekly sketches of what was happening under the skin of South Africa's first democratic Parliament and rubbed shoulders with the diverse leadership of what was to become known as, in Archbishop Desmond Tutu's words, the "rainbow nation". Tutu also makes an appearance in this book, one of a few leaders who was not representing a political party, along with the academic and intellectual Njabulo Ndebele, and the non-partisan minister of finance under Mandela, banker Chris Liebenberg.

It is these stories, once published but now mostly forgotten, that are included in this volume. I like to think I wrote these columns with humour, a sharp eye for detail and with a fairness that makes them an authentic and entertaining account of South Africa's story.

Professor Kader Asmal, law professor, founder of the Irish anti-apartheid movement and a cabinet minister in Mandela's first administration and in Mbeki's, approached me to help him write his memoirs (published by Jacana as *Kader Asmal Politics in my Blood*). This was in spite of the fact that my reportage and columns were often very critical of his policies, particularly when he served as Minister of Education. Later, after he had retired from public office, he told me, "Adrian, you were right! My hands were bound by the democratic decision-making practice of the African National Congress. Once a policy was agreed, I had no choice. But I disagreed with the policy from time to time and you were right to criticise it and me".

Though I got to know, and even became fond of, many of the figures who populate this book, I was never once accused by any one of them, from any party, of being unfair or untruthful or harbouring any kind of agenda other than to tell it as I saw it. I like to believe the stories and columns in this book are as fair, truthful and objective an account as it is possible to have of this extraordinary moment in South African history and of the people who were involved in it.

I have published this collection because I feel it is important that this account is made available for a greater understanding of the challenges and successes of a remarkable time. I feel hugely privileged to have been a witness to the events that are described in these pages and to have spent time with these extraordinary people just as I feel it is necessary to make this material available once more in an accessible, consolidated format.

This book consists of columns, feature articles, news stories and opinion pieces that I wrote during the period 1994 to 2001, from Mandela's inauguration as president deep into the following Mbeki administration. It was a hugely important period in which the entire legislative and constitutional landscape of South Africa was re-shaped. The articles appeared in a number of publications including *Publico* newspaper in Lisbon, the *Cape Argus*, *Drum* magazine, the *Saturday Star*, the *Sunday Independent, UPI* and *Business Day* newspaper, among others. Here they are gathered together for the first time and I hope will serve some purpose for readers and researchers in the future.

Adrian Hadland
Stirling, 2025

CONTENTS

ACKNOWLEDGMENTS

I have been fortunate to work with some extraordinary editors over the years who collectively gave me the space, literally and metaphorically, to tell South Africa's story the best way I could. Anton Harber and Irwin Manoim gave me my first job in journalism straight out of university at the pioneering anti-apartheid newspaper *The Weekly Mail* and were both inspirational and committed to the principles and practice of fine journalism. Jim Jones at *Business Day* offered me a post as a local government reporter just as I was looking for an opportunity to return to South Africa after finishing my Masters at Oxford. Promoted to Pretoria Bureau Chief, Jones demanded I submit extravagant expenses claims to match my instructions to wine and dine the entire diplomatic corps and the full spectrum of the country's political leadership. I tried my best not to disappoint. The programme of lunches, dinners and cocktail parties gave me an enviable contact list and a flow of exclusive stories that landed me in Parliament as a frontline writer for one of South Africa's most respected newspapers.

I arrived in Parliament during the final term of South Africa's last apartheid government, covered Nelson Mandela's election and his first and only term as president and was still in the press gallery three elections later. I was hired by Shaun Johnson, the editor of the newly created *Sunday Independent* to be the paper's Senior Writer. Shaun was a journalistic phenomenon who made a huge contribution to the narrative that accompanied South Africa's transition from conflicted, violent outcast to celebrated pioneer. He set out to showcase my writing and agreed to every opportunity that allowed me the space to show what I could do. Shaun's successor, John Battersby, was an equally dedicated editor who agreed I could take a year's leave to cover the Hong Kong handover in 1997, fulfilling a lifelong dream. I want to acknowledge Moegsien Williams who hired me as his Political Editor at the *Cape Argus*. Every morning, as I started to gather my thoughts for that day's editorial, he would urge me to add "peri-peri", to make it as spicey and controversial as possible.

Not one of these editors ever told me what to write, leaned on me to change my opinion or instructed me with whom or on what issue I wanted to focus. I believe South Africa's political press corps played a significant role in the country's transition to democracy: informing, communicating, testing ideas, criticising, supporting and restraining where necessary throughout one of humankind's most important experiments in reconciliation, forgiveness and the restoration of human rights.

Finally, I want to acknowledge photographer Anton Hammerl. Anton was a brilliant, compassionate, collegial, and generous photographer who gave his life to his work. The photo on the back cover of this book that he took of me having a laugh with Mandela was never intended to be published anywhere, it was just a gift that he took and printed for me as a token of an extraordinary day. That was typical of Anton, to be thinking of others even as he was going about his business. I have made a contribution to the Committee for the Protection of Journalists, who do amazing work looking after journalists in trouble, as a tribute to Anton's life and as a thank you for the use of this intimate, precious image.

1 FAREWELL APARTHEID

May 11 1994

South Africans should forget the past and work together to build a great country, President Nelson Mandela told an excited, cheering crowd of 60,000 people attending his inauguration at the Union Buildings in Pretoria yesterday.

Before starting his speech to the people gathered on the Botha lawn, Mandela danced briefly to the music of the African Jazz Pioneers, and the crowd danced delightedly with him.

In a carnival atmosphere, a group of youths ran across the lawn holding aloft a coffin with "*hamba kahle* apartheid" ("farewell apartheid") painted on the side.

The new president asked the nation to pray for his government, support it and wish it well. "That's all we need to secure your future," he said.

He and his two deputies, Thabo Mbeki and FW De Klerk, had long ago committed themselves to working for a better country, Mandela said.

Earlier, after he had taken his oath of office, Mandela told almost 60 heads of state, royalty and 6,000 other dignitaries that South Africa, the "rainbow nation", had at last achieved its political emancipation.

"Today all of us, by our presence here and by our celebrations in other parts of our country, confer glory and hope to newborn liberty."

Preceded by two traditional praise singers, Mandela climbed to the podium to a standing ovation. He paid special tribute to De Klerk who, with Mbeki, was sworn in as Deputy President.

In his address, he said that for the millions of South Africans who had suffered under apartheid and who went to the polls to elect a government of their own choice "today is a wonderful day indeed. It is a realisation of our dreams for which we have prayed so hard and so long."

"Let us forget the past. What is past is past," Mandela said in a continuation of the theme of reconciliation in recent speeches.

"The time for the healing of the wounds has come. The moment to bridge the chasms that divide us has come. The time to build is upon us."

As a token of its commitment to South Africa's renewal, Mandela said government would urgently "address the issue of amnesty for various categories of our people who are currently serving terms of imprisonment."

Mandela urged support and assistance from the representatives of foreign countries, who included Cuba's Fidel Castro and US Vice President Al Gore.

"We trust that you will continue to stand by us as we tackle the challenges of building peace, prosperity, non-sexism, non-racialism and democracy."

The people of South Africa felt they had been taken back into the "bosom of humanity" where they were no longer perceived as outlaws and skunks.

Of his election as president, Mandela said he was "both humbled and elated" but added that much still had to be done on the road to freedom. "We pledge ourselves to liberate all our people from the continuing bondage of poverty, deprivation, suffering, gender and other discrimination."

Mandela vowed that "never, never, and never again shall it be that this beautiful land will experience the oppression of one by another".

In dedicating the ceremony to those who had sacrificed their lives in the cause of a free South Africa, the new President said "their dreams had become reality. Freedom is their reward".

Mandela said hope had been implanted into the breasts of millions of people. "We enter into a covenant that we shall build the society in which all South Africans, black and white, will be able to walk tall, without any fear in their hearts, assured of their inalienable right to human dignity." South Africa would become a "rainbow nation at peace with itself and the world".

Later, in his third address of the day, at the VIP luncheon at the Presidency, Mandela said the new government would rely on persuasion and not the brute force of the past to rebuild the nation.

He and De Klerk had worked behind the scenes often in the past four years to ensure the negotiated and peaceful end to the brutality of apartheid.

It was a persuasive force, built on a common loyalty to and love for South Africa that would reconcile the country. The speech received a standing ovation from the members of more than 180 national delegations gathered to celebrate his inauguration.

2 THE SEARCH FOR TRUTH

March 1 1995

Day by day, details of the conspiracy and death, the deception, torture and extravagant human rights abuse characterising our violent heritage seep into the public domain.

From the revelations of superspy Craig Williamson to the evidence of the Eugene de Kock trial, from allegations in Parliament of state projects inciting "black on black" violence to lingering suspicions of atrocities in ANC camps, the truth is emerging from the shadows.

"Truth is on the march," wrote Emile Zola at the time of the Dreyfuss affair. "Nothing can stop it now".

But truth, as is being realised by legislators pondering the myriad clauses and ambitious aims of the Promotion of National Unity and Reconciliation Bill, is a far more complex and elusive affair than the bland statement of fact.

Truth implicates, accuses, saddens, and angers. The leaders of several minority parties, including the NP and the Inkatha Freedom Party, have even suggested the establishment of a truth commission will lead to vengeance, discrimination and renewed political conflict.

Somehow, the national consciousness must speedily yet thoroughly be purged of the poisonous past while laying a basis for reconciliation and nation-building.

Following the public participation process, it is now up to about 50 members of the National Assembly and Senate justice committees who begin this week to iron out the glitches in the legislation in a bid to create a process in which the perpetrators and victims of human rights violations will feel comfortable bearing the pain and excesses of the past.

It is likely, judging from submissions and testimonies given to parliamentary justice committees, that all truth commission hearings - whether of the commission itself or of its human rights, reparations, and amnesty committees - will be held in public.

The commission will be given scope to rule that certain hearings are conducted "in camera" if there is a genuine threat to life or state security matters are at stake.

It remains to be seen whether this will be enough to entice "third force" operatives to tell their stories. The Cabinet, which deliberately added the secrecy clause into the Bill at the NP's insistence, will still have to agree to this along with other political compromises inevitably adopted by the justice committees.

But the fact that there will have to be compromises indicates that there will be losers in the truth commission process. The commission cannot afford, nor is it likely, to grant amnesty to every person who claims to have committed offences for political motives.

Aside from this being contrary to international law, which rules that blanket amnesties may not be awarded to human rights abusers, universal absolution will set in place dangerous precedents which militate against the effective functioning of South Africa's criminal justice system.

Or so argues Justice Minister Dullah Omar who has stressed repeatedly that what happens in the truth commission will have "direct relevance" to crime and the rule of law in this country.

At the conclusion of the truth commission's deliberations, South Africa's population must be in no doubt that every crime committed from the cut-off date onwards - whether motivated by avarice or politics - will be prosecuted. This will be difficult to achieve if every human rights abuser is pardoned or if the prospect of amnesty is left open-ended for future recourse by devious villains.

This objective is also arguably complicated by the final clause of the interim constitution which states that "amnesty shall be granted" for offences associated with political objectives and committed in the course of the conflicts of the past.

The clause then goes on to say that a law will be passed providing for the mechanisms, criteria and procedures, including tribunals, through which such amnesty shall be dealt with "at any time after the law has been passed".

The danger, as NP justice spokesman Danie Schutte has argued, is that this implies the availability of amnesty for "political crimes" in perpetuity. This is part, too, of the debate over the amnesty cut-off date given in the Bill, and the interim constitution, as December 5 1993.

If the date is changed to May 10 last year, which is recommended by several parties including the AWB, the impression might be given that government is infinitely flexible.

If the cut-off date is not changed, about 200 "political prisoners" will remain in their cells - most of them from Inkatha, the PAC and the right wing - aggrieved and bitter.

There is, however, no commonly accepted or internationally recognised definition of what constitutes a political crime or even what makes a political prisoner.

The draft legislation does attempt to set out criteria for determining whether an act or crime was committed with political objectives in mind.

In broad terms, the Bill suggests that an act "associated with a political objective" by a member of either a "publicly known political organisation or liberation movement" or someone acting on behalf of the state is eligible for amnesty.

Several legal, political, and human rights bodies have argued the terms "associated with" and "publicly known" are too woolly to be valid.

Perhaps the most controversial definition in the Bill is the statement that crimes undertaken where "no reasonable relationship exists between the act committed and the objective pursued" cannot be considered political.

Given this basis, and the fact of its inclusion in the Bill, where do the APLA soldiers who bombed the Heidelberg Tavern stand, not to mention many other examples of acts undertaken by both the security forces and the liberation armies?

A host of other issues have still to be ironed out by legislators before truth commissioners can be appointed and the work of truth and reconciliation begun.

These include the question of the composition of the commission, the access of victims to civil claims against perpetrators, the admissibility in law courts of evidence heard by the commission, levels of compensation, the degree of collective responsibility by political and military leaders, the protection of witnesses, the question as to whether violators should be convicted before receiving amnesty or whether amnesty should be awarded in lieu of conviction, and the applicability of various constitutional rights.

All this is complicated by Inkatha leader Mangosuthu Buthelezi's recent rejection of the commission as an "evil institution" and, presumably, his party's subsequent opposition to the Bill in its entirety.

The 50-odd legislators currently sifting through the clauses, inferences and rights contained in the Bill face an awesome task under urgent time constraints. Their success or failure, however, could have major implications for South Africa's level of political conflict and the sanctity of its criminal justice system.

3 CHRISTMAS WITH MANDELA

December 25 1995

It is a little before five in the morning and Nelson Mandela is dressed to walk the hills in the dark, moist weather.

The sun is scarcely an orange smudge above the misty Transkei valleys of his birthplace, but Mandela has a lot of ground to cover.

He chooses a different direction each day, sometimes south to the village of Mvezo on the banks of the Bashe River, where he was born; sometimes toward Mqhekezweni, the Great Place, formerly the residence of Chief Jongintaba Dalindyebo, where Mandela lived for the 10 years prior to his circumcision.

As he walks, the people in the scattered hamlets come hailing him with calls of "Madiba", "Nkosi" or "Dada". They take his hand in theirs, women and children looking away in the traditional sign of respect.

They chat for a few moments before he walks on through the mist or rain that quickly rolls across the shallow hills.

The children rush to greet him, pushing their small hands into his boxer's paws, laughing. He asks each of them their name and, usually, about their schoolwork.

For a few precious weeks each year, the South African president returns to

Qunu, the place of his childhood.

"It becomes important, the older you get, to return to places where you have wonderful recollections," he says. "This is really home".

It was in the fields surrounding the village of Qunu, just 35km southeast of Umtata in the Eastern Cape, that Mandela had some of his most formative experiences. Here, he has built an exact replica of the house in the grounds of the Victor Verster Prison in Paarl where he spent the last of his 27 years in prison.

It was this house, guarded by a few bored warders (they became bored when they realised he wouldn't try to escape, he says) that he enjoyed his first moments in almost three decades of being "practically free".

For this reason, the house has pleasant memories and so has been rebuilt in the place closest to his heart. When its rooms are filled with his grandchildren and people from the surrounding villages have gathered in his garden to feast, then he is truly a happy man.

As he walks, the fond memories come flooding back: the big boulder he used to slide down as a child, his first school, the trading store where he first saw white people, the hut he used to share with his childhood friend, Justice, son of Dalindyebo.

But it is not all sweet recollection and misty-eyed reminiscence. The abject poverty of many of these people, the brackish drinking water, the smoking cow dung they use to cook their meals and scarcely heat their homes - all this saddens him deeply and is a clear reminder of the awesome responsibilities he now holds towards them and many others.

"When you see the children, the way they are dressed, completely emaciated, you are really moved," he says. "You feel the indescribable pain of poverty and responsibility".

At one village, an impromptu meeting is held with children scattering off to round up still dozing or working adults. Thirty or forty people are gathered by the time the chief begins his speech. "Madiba, we are very proud you grew up here," he says, a second elder translating. "Whenever we see you putting your feet in our soil it gives us great hope".

One of Mandela's fondest memories is of the tales he used to hear while living at Dalindyebo's kraal in Mqhekezweni. It is not surprising, then, that Mandela too likes to tell a good tale or two in the autumn of a remarkable life.

But the stories of the latest leader of the Madiba clan are far more international than ever they were at Dalindyebo's kraal. He now speaks of US President Bill Clinton and of the American leader's somewhat testy relationship with Cuba's Fidel Castro and Palestinian leader Yasser Arafat; he chuckles over the repeated bearhugs dished out by Russian President Boris Yeltsin. He describes former British Prime Minister Margaret Thatcher's gentleness and motherliness and her Labour Party opponent Neil Kinnock's shock at the description. He tells of French premier Jacques Chirac's support and frankness and, off the record, of the various idiosyncrasies of some of South Africa's better-known leaders.

As we round the crest of a hill, his homestead is nestled some 500m below in a verdant valley. The brick house, of jail staff quarters design, is faintly incongruous with the grass roofs and mud walls of his neighbours. But the Christmas lights on the young pine trees leading to his front door, the smoke from an outside fire curling up into the morning sky and the two yellow marquees in the back garden are a welcoming prospect.

On Christmas morning, anyone who lives within walking distance of the Mandela kraal is invited to a two-day feast. Sixteen sheep and an ox are slaughtered for an expected 600 guests. Mandela's great-grandaughter, Rochelle, has been up all night wrapping presents. As usual, the children come first; the adults will only eat once the children have been fed. ("There is brandy for the old ones later if the food has run out," he says).

As he walks down the hill homewards, alongside the main road from Umtata to East London, people wave and shout from their cars. Some stop and come over to introduce themselves.

It has been one of the disadvantages of his fame and renown - the lack of privacy, he says. In 1984, while serving time on Robben Island, he was placed in isolation. Though he could meet the other prisoners occasionally, he became used to living alone. It is partly for this reason that he no longer holidays at the game farms so strongly recommended by Deputy President Thabo Mbeki and Jakes Gerwel, the cabinet secretary.

On this day, there is time before the feast begins and the neighbours start to show-up in their Sunday best, for a quick motorised tour of the outlying districts and villages he hasn't had time to reach on foot.

But first a cup of tea, a game with the grandchildren, and a glance at the Sunday papers. Kicking off his muddy shoes in the doorway of his kitchen, with the hills of Qunu partly obscured by the early morning mist, he is home, truly home.

4 MANDELA AND DE KLERK'S TEMPESTUOUS RELATIONSHIP

October 8 1995

If ever there was a symbol of the birth of the new South Africa, and of its subsequent trials and tribulations, it is the personal relationship between Nelson Mandela and FW de Klerk.

It has been an epic affair: tumultuous, angry, respectful, bitter, and forgiving. It has run the gamut of emotions from triumph to despair, and by surviving it has inspired the nation and intoxicated the world.

Following the latest recent spat in downtown Johannesburg on a warm September night, it is easy to forget how frequently the two statesmen have clashed - and how, usually sooner rather than later, they have returned to a comfortable orbit.

Countless times, fizzing, long-distance telephone calls or one-on-one meetings between the two have served to avert what appeared to be an imminent national disaster ("The all-important summit on violence," the *Star* reported in September 1992, "has been rescued by personal contact between President De Klerk and ANC leader Nelson Mandela") just as frequently as they have disdained each other with petulance and irritability ("President De Klerk and ANC leader Nelson Mandela had an ugly public clash yesterday," the *Star* reported from Philadelphia in July 1993).

As we wait now to see the fall-out settle from this latest episode, which De Klerk described this week as the emergence of "fundamental philosophical differences", it is worth reminding both, and the nation, of the words spoken by De Klerk to Mandela during his Nobel prize acceptance speech in December 1993:

"We will be called upon often to rise above our differences and find ways of bridging them and finding consensus. We must make reconciliation work. We cannot build the future on hate and retribution. We can build the future only if we put the past behind us."

And to quote to Mandela's words to De Klerk, taken from the famous live television pre-election debate: "I am proud to hold your hand. Let us go forward together, let us work together to end division and suspicion."

None would argue the point that both men have been the subject to the whims of political and natural forces beyond their control or ken. De Klerk has had to contend with the bitter paradox of being both deputy president and opposition party leader. Mandela has had to ride the accusations of excessive latitude toward the former oppressors while feeding the expectations of a newly enfranchised populace.

Throw into the pot the Bisho and Sebokeng massacres, a referendum, and a general election together with all the other slings and arrows of a nation in transition, and it is extraordinary that they are still even talking to each other.

But it is worth gazing back briefly at some of the high and low points of the relationship and to put the current dispute in context.

Within hours of his release in February 1990, Mandela's comments from the balcony at the Grand Parade in Cape Town, particularly on the continuation of the armed struggle, alarmed De Klerk. This was despite Mandela calling De Klerk a man of integrity and honour.

Matters came to a head in December that year at the opening session of the Convention for a Democratic South Africa (Codesa). In what pundits described as "an extraordinary gloves-off exchange" that stunned delegates and dignitaries, De Klerk issued an ultimatum to the ANC to dismantle its armed wing. Mandela assumed the platform and harangued De Klerk for half an hour.

"He can do what he likes," Mandela told the gathering. "We are not going to disband Umkhonto weSizwe."

In April 1992, a new rumpus erupted when Mandela accused De Klerk of being directly involved in the violence sweeping the country. Laws permitting the carrying of traditional weapons had given certain parties within the country free rein to slaughter ANC members, Mandela argued.

"When De Klerk unbanned the ANC, shortly thereafter he authorised the carrying of these dangerous weapons ... He was giving capacity to certain people, to certain organisations, to carry weapons of death and to murder innocent people."

By September 1992, the cordial relations between the two men, "which had been in tatters for months" had been restored and full bilateral negotiations at the World Trade Centre in Kempton Park were resumed.

However, a squabble over sanctions caused further difficulties a few months later while the two leaders were visiting the United States to receive their Philadelphia Liberty medals. The *Washington Post*, noting that both men studiously avoided each other during the trip, carried the headline: "De Klerk and Mandela, Alone Together".

Though this was soon sorted out, a South African Defence Force raid on Umtata in late 1993 caused great friction, with Mandela accusing De Klerk of terrorism before their joint award of the Nobel peace prize caused gushings of mutual admiration.

"Whatever criticisms I have against Mr De Klerk ... it would not have been possible for us to reach this stage without his contribution. He has played an important role," Mandela told guests at the Oslo ceremony.

The spirit of this moment was to be carried through to the "great debate" when De Klerk and Mandela had their first live debate on television. In an inspired moment, Mandela reached out his hand to De Klerk. "I am proud to hold your hand," Mandela told his old adversary.

With the successful conclusion of the April 27 1994 election, more words of gratitude were forthcoming. De Klerk's speech at National Party headquarters, in which he conceded defeat, was a classic gesture of reconciliation.

"During the past four years we have proved that we can work together. Despite our differences, our relationship has become a symbol of the ability of South Africans from widely different backgrounds to co-operate in the national interest," he said.

Mandela was equally magnanimous, calling De Klerk during his inauguration speech "one of the greatest sons of Africa" and a man of great personal courage and integrity.

Since then the dynamics of the government of national unity have apparently taken their toll, with new splits and new starts characterising the on-off relationship.

With such a history, however, there is surely little doubt that the De Klerk-Mandela epic has a good few episodes left to run.

5 THE YOUNG LIONS OF DOUGLAS

October 15, 1995

Prince Khoza just couldn't stop attracting attention during the struggle days of the 1980s. As a Communist Party leader and civic activist, he stuck out in small but affluent Northern Cape community of Douglas like the towering grain silo on the outskirts of town.

His comings and goings, speeches and activities were noted and observed by the small but efficient local constabulary as easily as the silver-grey dust cloud billowing behind the Campbell school bus.

In a community of 12,000 people, carefully segregated into the white town of Douglas, the black township of Bongani and the coloured area of Breipaal, there are just not that many places to hide.

He was arrested and detained 17 times.

He and his comrade colleagues from Bongani and Breipaal represent everything the stolidly conservative farmers and white residents of Douglas despised and feared about the liberation struggle.

Apart from their more overtly political activities and their sympathy with communist principles and objectives, they initiated the rates and services boycott in 1989 which emptied the town coffers by bringing payments tumbling to less than three percent of township residents.

Now Khoza is one of the ANC's major candidates in the local government elections. There is more than an even chance, given the range of portfolios he holds in political and civic organisations, together with the expected margin of victory for the ANC, that from November 1 he will be the town's mayor.

At 35, Khoza is one of the veterans of the ANC's team of candidates in Douglas's four wards.

Leroy Adams is barely 22, Thapelo Makabe and Benjamin Sehwelo are 26 and Regina Mantie is 21. They are the young lions of Douglas and they intend ringing the changes in the coming months.

The contrast with the current order is all the starker in view of the nature of the economy and the political conservativism of Douglas.

The Northern Cape is characterised by heartbreaking aridity and vast swathes of rugged, dusty veld. It's hard, harsh land pocked by anthills, thorntrees and isolated settlements of people huddled around wells and streams.

"There's no drought here," says one resident. "It never has rained here, and it never will."

In this barren landscape, water truly is the source of life. And in this, Douglas has been doubly blessed. Just west of the town occurs what townsfolk call "the confluence". "Have you been to see the confluence?" they ask of newcomers. "It's beautiful". Signs to the confluence are scattered about the town's neat business district and at each of the major intersections.

The confluence is the point at which the great Vaal and Orange rivers join. The quantities of fresh water emanating from such a union have been the lifeblood of the town and the source of its wealth and development.

Unlike most of Douglas's sister towns across the arid plains, anything can be grown near the confluence. Vineyards, maize, vegetables and fruit trees thrive in the rich soil.

"The only things we don't grow in Douglas are coffee, sugar cane and bananas," says Khoza proudly. "And we are having talks at the moment about building a sugar plant."

The Mercedes and BMW cars parked in the shade of palm and willow trees are indicative of kind of wealth such access to water and fertile land has generated over the years. Such prosperity has also fostered a political loyalty to the National Party, which has held sway over the town's council for many years. The NP has also had significant levels of support among the town's coloured residents.

The clash between the old and new, between the tradition and conservatism of the *ancien régime* and the radical idealism of the young lions could hardly be more evident.

It is the new confluence. Gradually the residents of Douglas are becoming conscious that the energies deriving from such a union could yet propel the town into a new era of growth and prosperity.

"We want to build the rainbow nation right here in Douglas," says Khoza.

There is, of course, suspicion and distrust to overcome in both communities. The older generation in Bongani and Breipaal have had to be convinced that councillors with an average age in the early twenties could be trusted to represent their interests, says prospective councillor Leroy Adams, who is 22. "The elderly people have difficulty in understanding this system of negotiation. But they do understand that negotiation, in which the young have skills and experience, has the potential to lift the communities out of the mess they are in."

The ward and proportional representation conferences held in Douglas in July this year, at which the ANC's prospective candidates were voted for and named, signalled an emphatic backing for the new generation.

"They showed us that they trusted us."

While most ordinary residents understand the importance of the local elections, apathy levels are still high, says Makabe.

But the candidates are confident that door-to-door canvassing will pay off and that a substantial proportion of the Breipaal residents who voted NP in the last election will switch their loyalties on November 1.

Meanwhile, there has been some smoothing of feathers in the white community too. A minor dispute erupted recently when Freedom Front canvassers allegedly removed ANC election posters in town and replaced them with their own.

Weekly meetings have been taking place between the ANC candidates and the local ratepayers' association, says Khoza.

"We talk with them every week. If you don't talk to them, you don't know what their fears are."

Says Makabe: "They are worried they will be excluded, so we get together and share ideas. We keep telling them they have nothing to fear."

As a sign of their commitment to the town, the ANC candidates have been pushing residents to resume payment of services and rates. While unemployment levels are high and the average wage on a Douglas farm amounts to R10 a day, the payment rate is up to 60 percent, says Khoza. "They are trying their level best".

Of the police who harassed him with such regularity, Khoza says attitudes are beginning to adapt to the new times. As the newly appointed chairman of the police community forum, few know the ins and outs of law enforcement procedures better than he.

"Things are changing very much," he says. "Every day they are better."

Though the election is only in a few weeks' time, the confluence has begun. The old and the new have begun to find each other.

The surging currents of attitude and history are beginning to mingle and, in so doing, are bringing the people of Douglas to realise that their destinies are bound as inextricably as the waters of the Vaal and the Orange.

6 SYDNEY MUFAMADI'S DETECTIVES GET DOWN TO WORK

February 4 1996

It is an unassuming house from the outside. The grass is long and unkempt. Paint is peeling off the walls. A To Let sign is still standing at an angle on the scruffy, tousled rectangle of front lawn.

Shoulder to shoulder with a locksmith, a bottlestore and a second-hand car dealership in the heart of the south coast town of Port Shepstone, few would, or do, give No 15 a second glance.

But, inside, concealed by the Indian Ocean spray that gathers on the windowpanes and by the government issue blinds that absorb the summer glare, the cream of South Africa's investigative talent is engaged in an exercise that could yet rip the heart out of political violence in KwaZulu-Natal.

Sydney Mufamadi, the safety and security minister, appointed the special investigation unit last year. It is headed by Bushie Engelbrecht and is one of the largest and most talented teams of special detectives ever assembled in South Africa.

Only the team put together to track down the infamous Station Strangler, who murdered 22 young boys on the Cape Flats in the early 1990s, compares in size to the one now operating out of the nondescript house.

At its peak, which was only for a week or two, the Strangler team had 70 detectives. The special investigation team in Port Shepstone is 36 strong, going into its second month, and is growing all the time as the trail warms up and the quarry is separated from the pack.

This week, the team arrested six people in connection with several massacres that took place in KwaZulu-Natal in December last year. Further arrests are expected.

A closer look at No 15 begins to betray what is happening within its walls. There are a half-dozen brand-new air conditioners screwed on to the peeling facade to fend off the numbing south coast humidity.

The vehicles, mostly bakkies[1], that drive up and down the steep driveway in a constant relay have number plates from across the country and they bristle with antennae.

Extremely large men, with what look like artillery pieces strapped to their hips, shuffle in and out.

Inside, the pace is frenetic.

People - none in uniform but all with that quintessential, cross-cultural, and cross-national cop look - come and go bearing files and papers.

In one room, detectives sit at computer terminals, their thick fingers drumming fragile plastic keyboards, their faces etched with deep concentration. In another, the *modus operandi* and other case details have been set out in columns on a white board.

Engelbrecht is a 29-year veteran of the police force and a stalwart of the Durban riot investigation unit. He was a brigadier before ranks in the police force were changed to civilian equivalents. Now he is a director.

He and his team must find those responsible for three brutal massacres that

---

[1] Pick-up or open-backed truck

took place in the lower south coast region of KwaZulu-Natal last year.

The last of these was the infamous Shobashabane massacre in which 19 people were killed and dozens more injured.

The team includes Zulu speakers and has been divided into five groups. They all have detailed explanations of how the witness protection programme operates and this has tested the team's investigative work.

Nine witnesses have taken advantage of the protection programme and will testify when the cases reach court.

But the spectre of police complicity has made the team's task that much more difficult. Links between current cases and older ones keep turning up. But the keeping and updating of thousands of case dockets has been sloppy and, in some cases, deliberately confused.

Criminals who have sought to take advantage of the political conflict have complicated the investigation. A local IFP leader said the Shobashabane massacre was sparked by the hijacking of a truck carrying a year's supply of *stokvel* supplies.

The local tradition of knocking down a house in which a murder or cruelty has transpired, and particularly those huts with blood smeared on their walls, has also made the search for clues more difficult.

Engelbrecht is confident that more arrests will be made soon, and few residents or politicians doubt the work of the team will be crucial in the bid to stem political violence in the province.

But for now, the team members must leave the sanctity and coolness of their peeling headquarters, climb into their bakkies, and head off once more into the field.

7 CHRIS LIEBENBERG NEVER HECKLES

March 10 1996

[Mandela's first minister of finance, Chris Liebenberg, was a non-partisan, Harvard-educated banker pulled from industry to quieten international and domestic concerns about a lack of financial experience among the ANC's leadership. He served as minister of finance from September 1994 to April 1996.]

He usually sits on his own, on the opposition side of the National Assembly, next to the small PAC contingent.

With his precisely combed silver hair and large steel-rimmed glasses, his freshly pressed suits, striped banker shirts and frowns of concentration, he is as easily identifiable as he is impeccably aloof.

He is Chris Liebeberg, minister of finance, and an apparent anachronism in the charged atmosphere that is Parliament.

He never heckles, "vivas" or "hoor hoors"; doesn't nod off or read the papers. He is uncomfortable in the limelight, a behind-the-scenes man happier surrounded by facts and figures than by hype and bluster.

He is also the only MP who was not elected and who represents no political party. The constitution had to be changed for him to assume his cabinet position and it is unlikely that after 1999 there will be a non-partisan finance minister at all.

On Wednesday afternoon this week, the 61-year-old former banker will climb up to the podium to present to the nation one of the last budgets of its kind.

Not only will Liebenberg be allowed to let a hint of his own vision enter the public domain, now that the apartheid legacy is in retreat, but the very nature of the budget is in the process of radical transformation.

After next year, for instance, it is unlikely to be presented in March, for Parliament, and in particular the finance committee, to play a more active role.

As Liebenberg explained in a pre-session briefing, "by presenting the budget on March 13 coming into effect on April 1, there is really very little time for Parliament to reject the budget, for instance. So, we need to change that cycle to bring Parliament into the process much more effectively."

Liebenberg has far-reaching plans for the budgetary process, and for government financing in general. In order to address problems stemming from the huge sums of money which are rolled over each year in many departments, government's accounting will be changed, Liebenberg hopes, from cash accounting to an accrual system.

A more sophisticated debt management system operation, looking in particular at liability, asset, risk and cash management, will be established in a bid to make more efficient government's use of funds.

Further changes, and 24 are being investigated currently, include the entrenchment of modern management practices into government policy. More attention will be paid to return on assets, return on investments and on equity as well as on dividend policy.

The country, in other words, will be run more like a corporation than a quango. This is the heart of Liebenberg's vision.

It is an initiative Liebenberg's deputy Alec Erwin calls "financial engineering".

The pillars of Liebenberg's endeavour are the so-called "six-pack" of objectives approved by cabinet last year: belt tightening through improved financial management; budget reform; the restructuring of state assets; reform of the public service; enhancement of provincial financial relations; and, boosting internal monitoring.

And it is this that forms the context for the 1996-7 budget.

Though this is a "boom budget" - the growth rate being higher and inflation lower than at any time during the past 10 years - the belt-tightening principle will prevent any expansionary extravagance.

Keeping inflation, government consumption expenditure and state debt down are "fundamentals", says Liebenberg.

But money will have to be found to pay for new items such as the R250-million a year required for "struggle" pensions[2] and to ease the high tax burden on low- and middle-income earners.

The smart money says some of this will come from retirement funds, without damaging the golden egg of contractual savings, probably in the form of closed loopholes and ended exemptions.

The potential for controversy inherent in raising VAT will probably scare Liebenberg off. He might think he can get away with a one-point hike or expand the VAT net to include some financial services.

A radical and overdue overhaul of the revenue and excise operations will also contribute to the state coffers, though prudence dictates a conservative estimate of new income and little instant relief in other areas.

Pundits have also suggested that top tax brackets will be changed and that the top marginal tax rate and possibly death duties will be raised. There might be an increase in excise duty on some consumer products, particularly the usual

[2] 'Struggle pensions' refers to the provision in South Africa's constitution for the distribution of payments to "persons or their dependents who made sacrifices or who have served the public interest in the establishment of a democratic constitutional order".

targets of tobacco and booze. The one percent marketable securities tax could be abolished, and anti-avoidance procedures and fringe benefits abuse could be tightened.

However, Liebenberg has stressed that he is reluctant to impose taxes where vested or accumulated rights of individuals will be affected.

Though he is not the greatest orator of our times - and this is never more painfully obvious than during his epic budget speeches - Liebenberg exudes gravitas and prudence. He is not easily provoked, even when the currency is crashing on world markets.

For the first time, though, we can expect his signature to be firmly imprinted on the budget as he seeks to bring the standards and instruments of the private sector to bear on the finances of the nation.

8 TRUTH COMMISSION HEARS CHILLING FACTS

October 27 1996

They were known as the Sanhedrin and they held more power during the dark days of apartheid than perhaps anyone.

But what was once a court of justice in New Testament Jerusalem was something quite different and far more sinister in South Africa during the 1980s.

The Sanhedrin were the regional desk heads of South Africa's infamous policy security branch, the "backbone" of the state's fight against the liberation movements. Every day they would meet at the branch's headquarters in Pretoria to discuss events and plans, and to deliberate over lives and deaths.

Testimony at the Johannesburg City Hall this week by five former members of the Northern Transvaal division of the security branch seeking amnesty from the truth commission has shed new light on the workings and structure of the apartheid state's most feared organ.

The revelations, which had the former minister of law and order, Adriaan Vlok, and former commissioner of police, Johan van der Merwe, scurrying to apply for amnesty, were both chilling and damning.

"It is the time for truth. It is time for confession," the five's lawyer, Willem Britz, read out in their opening statement on Monday.

In attempting to fulfil the only two conditions for amnesty, full disclosure of acts committed and proof of the political nature of those acts, the five have begun to unravel the secrets of what Van der Merwe called the "shadowy and often murky world" of counter-revolution.

It was a world in which morality had long been overwhelmed, a world in which a war psychosis had taken root and in which actions were, in Van der Merwe's own words, "cold-blooded and murderous of nature".

This was the world of the security branch and the cutting edge of apartheid atrocities, the place at which the state became both enforcer and executioner.

According to one of the five, Brigadier Jack Cronje, a former Vlakplaas commander who headed the branch's Northern Transvaal division in the mid 1980s, the security police's capacity to collect information was "the best in the world".

Files on tens of thousands of activists and operatives were kept up to date daily both at the branch's 20 divisions and at headquarters, "Compol", the office of the commissioner of police.

A huge network of informers, marshalled by a combination of terror and financial reward, spanned the length and breadth of the country, feeding the force's 101 branches with a constant stream of information and tip-offs.

Many of the most effective informants, as well as the most brutal operatives, were former ANC or PAC fighters, called Askaris, who had been "turned" during interrogation.

The usual method of interrogation, according to Colonel Roelof Venter - one of the amnesty applicants who headed the security branch's interrogation division, called C2, for five years - was "to use violence, to humiliate people, to assault, to intimidate as a means of gaining information from them".

"Any effective method was acceptable in the context of war and the total onslaught," he told the truth commission's amnesty committee this week.

Behind him, a truth commission poster could as easily have been a comment on the branch's interrogation techniques: "The truth hurts but silence kills".

Some would speak after an hour, others after a few days, Venter told the commission. If the victim held out, the questioning and assaults would go on and on, day and night, for as long as it took.

Sometimes, if the information given was really useful, the victim would be killed to protect both the information and the person who had informed on him.

The security branch tapped phones, opened mail and mercilessly interrogated activists in the quest for information.

This data, together with news of branch actions and conditions on the ground, was relayed every morning to the branch's headquarters in Pretoria.

Here, the so-called Sanhedrin would mull over developments. Every month they would brief both the State Security Council, which consisted of top politicians and government officials, and the even more ominous group called the Counter Revolutionary Target Information Centre (or Trewits, as it was known by its Afrikaans acronym).

The latter, as was revealed for the first time this week, drew up monthly hit lists of activists both in South Africa and abroad who were to be killed.

Evidence given to the commission indicates that while Trewits meetings were secret, members of both the local Joint Control Centre and the State Security Council were aware of its activities.

But what had been a relatively efficient operation during the late 1970s and early 1980s began to crumble a few years later. In the face of mass resistance and following the intensification of both the armed struggle and the drive for ungovernability, the security branch simply could not keep up.

Under pressure from the politicians to keep a firm lid on the boiling populace, the branch resorted to ever more brutal methods.

Orders from the State Security Council that had once been specific became general and vague. They were often word-of-mouth instructions or, at best, communiques.

The order from the former law and order minister Adriaan Vlok, to destroy Khotso House in Johannesburg was given by word of mouth, just as Vlok had received the order orally from then state president PW Botha, according to Cronje.

Cronje gave one example of an order given to the Northern Transvaal branch: "Pretoria is burning, South Africa is burning. Bring the situation under control. It doesn't matter how".

At the time that greater demands were being placed on the security police, their effectiveness, together with the capacity of the state's overarching Joint Management System to contain "unrest", began to erode.

Government departments started to squabble amongst themselves for the right to lead the activities of the Joint Management System.

The level of support for the liberation armies among black communities meant information began to dry up while informants and police officers faced increasingly hostile conditions.

The imposition in 1985 of a state of emergency conferred on the police by its regulations, succeeded only in devolving these powers to places where accountability and transparency were as remote as the notion of minimal force.

"The enemy had to be halted at all costs. Our instructions were to bring the riots under control, and it didn't matter how," said Cronje. The law no longer mattered.

"Our people became confused. The distinction between legal and illegal became more and more blurred," said Van der Merwe.

In the state's determination to ride out the rising wave of resistance, it called on the police to cooperate with the army.

Police officers with experience of combat - and many had served either in Zimbabwe during the 1970s or with Koevoet in Namibia prior to independence - were told to work with the South African Defence Force's secret assault unit, the special forces.

"There was some disagreement and difficulties in co-operating with the SADF but we would have worked with military intelligence if we had to.

"We were not told to co-operate with military intelligence but with [the SADF's] special forces. Special forces were a combat group. The order was a direct instruction to get involved in a war, to become militarily engaged ... It was a military onslaught. It was a war."

Whether or not Judge Hassen Mall's Amnesty Committee accepts this and accepts too the notion that all five policemen have fully disclosed everything they know, will be key factors in determining what kind of role the past will play in their immediate and, perhaps, long-term future.

[Brigadier Jack Cronje, Colonel Roelof Venter, Warrant Officer Paul van Vuuren, Captain Jacques Hechter, and Captain Wouter Mentz were all granted amnesty.]

9 'HONOURABLE MEMBERS, YOUR CONDUCT IS DISGRACEFUL'

April 24 1998

"Sies! Sies!" shouts ANC MP Mavivi Myakayaka-Manzini, leaning over her pew in the National Assembly.

"What an ignoramus you are," Trevor Manuel, the finance minister, calls out to the hapless NP speaker.

"He looks like a boy in his grandfather's suit," a backbencher chips in.

And so the debate on the President's budget vote got under way this week to a chorus of rebukes, insults and interjections.

Little wonder that in his closing speech, President Nelson Mandela expressed what verged on bewilderment at the increasingly aggressive interchanges that have come to characterise our legislature.

Frene Ginwala, the Speaker of Parliament, was almost beside herself at times trying to control the mostly good-humoured rowdiness.

"Honourable members, your conduct is disgraceful," she railed after yelling "order" until she was almost hoarse. "Unless you control yourselves, we cannot have a debate."

Two weeks ago, Ginwala and a number of her colleagues visited the Swedish Parliament, the Riksdag.

The atmosphere in the Riksdag's debating chamber was solemn, dignified and generally co-operative. The multiparty South African group was impressed.

"It was remarkable how nice and quiet the house was," Ginwala noted wistfully on her return.

She was quickly reminded of how lively things can get closer to home.

The debate began calmly enough with Mandela issuing his usual appeal for co-operation from the opposition parties and a renewed dedication to the notion of a national consensus.

But traditionally the President's budget debate is open season for just about anything that MPs want to get off their chests.

A significant part of the debate this week was spent fighting off interjections, responding to previous remarks or waiting for the Speaker to control heckling opponents rather than making valid points.

In his opening address on Tuesday, Mandela said: "It is only too easy to stir up the baser feelings that exist in any society with a history such as ours.

"Worse still, it is only too easy to do this in a way that undermines our achievements in building national unity and enhancing the legitimacy of our national institutions ... It is much easier to destroy than to build."

Whether it was members' embarrassment at the sheer excesses of the preceding debate, the appeals of the president or the stern warnings from the whips, by the time Mandela closed the debate on Wednesday afternoon, an eerie calm had descended on the national assembly.

"We do need to ask ourselves whether we always conduct ourselves with the decorum that is appropriate to the highest institution of democracy," he said. "Do honourable members always behave in a way that shows respect for those who elected them; for the public who observe them through the media; for their colleagues; and for themselves?"

The answer to all four questions was apparently a resounding "no".

But the looming election means that debates in parliament are likely to remain closer to the Westminster model of raucous interjection than the Riksdag's calmer approach, a trend that Ginwala will surely rue.

10 THREE GENERALS IN THE DOCK

December 3 1995

Durban - There they are, as few could have imagined not so many years ago. Shoulder to shoulder in the dock: big Magnus Malan, hunched and austere; Kat Liebenberg, a muscle in his tanned cheek twitching throughout; Jannie Geldenhuys, blinking frequently and appearing older with every passing minute.

Three knuckles in the mailed fist of white domination, cramped and constrained now in a shabby Durban courtroom.

Seldom has Court Z of the Durban Regional Court been so packed. An assortment including lawyers, the odd politician and the press are crammed into the wooden benches of the public gallery.

Rapid reaction squad police bristle lethally - submachine guns with flashlights taped to the muzzles, teargas grenades, bandoliers of shotgun shells, walkie talkies, bullet-proof jackets, earpieces and enough Ramboesque equipment to capture the Comores - and wait bored as the scheduled starting time of 9am comes and goes.

Outside, a rusting water cannon is parked near the 12-storey courthouse. It is equipped with two tanks: one water and teargas, the other water and blue dye.

Inside, Tannie Sue, the long-serving court stenographer, leans her head on her hand and taps her fingers carelessly. Papers on the magistrate's bench flutter once on the breath of a silent gust.

Then suddenly, at about 9.15am, action in the sluggish humidity. Figures moving around behind misted glass walls, doors opening and closing down unseen corridors, a crash from the cells.

A court messenger arrives with a cardboard box and, pulling off the lid, begins to pile stapled documents on the U-shaped table in the heart of the courtroom: the indictments have finally arrived. Finally, seven men emerge from the steep stairwell. These are the Inkatha men, accused of carrying out the raid on the KwaMakhutha house on that fateful day in 1987.

Lawyers begin to pour into the amphitheatre. The defence: Klaus von Lieres und Wilkau, only recently Witwatersrand attorney-general, Inkatha parliamentarian and lawyer Koos van der Merwe; Sam Moritz - who will defend the bulk of the accused, including the generals - and the young bloods Jacky Singh and Patrick Falconer. A number of other legal advisers look for somewhere to sit.

The prosecution: KwaZulu-Natal attorney-general Tim McNally is not here but his deputy, Benny Schoenfeldt, takes the reins; senior public prosecutor Barend Groen mills around with a clipboard. There is commotion below and the 13 accused, led by Malan, climb up.

Peering over the scuffed panels surrounding the stairwell, I see a line of pale faces gazing upwards. It is a moment of great vulnerability: bravado drains away under the gravity of a box full of indictments and the focus of a room full of eyes.

They are led straight out, again behind glass, returning to take their seats in two rows, squashed and undignified.

All rise as the magistrate JJ Augustyn, enters. He cannot contain a wry, bemused expression. Before him is a circus.

Countless lawyers move around like dodgem cars; 20 defendants sit as if numbed by Valium. The public gallery heaves with activity.

Following the introduction of counsel, Maritz and then Von Lieres warm to their task of extracting kinder bail conditions from the state. Once the judge has ruled in favour of the defence's two applications, the indictment proceeds. The name of each of the accused is read out and a copy of the document is handed to them.

The magistrate warns the 20 to appear again on March 4 in Durban's Supreme Court and bustle in Court Z dissipates into the busy 12th floor of the courthouse and then into the bright summer sunshine of Durban on the first day of December.

(Malan and the other accused were bailed and ordered to appear in court again on 1 December 1995. A seven-month trial then ensued which exacerbated racial tensions in South Africa. All the accused were eventually acquitted.)

11 FW DE KLERK: 'LET'S LOOK FORWARD, NOT BACK'

December 24, 1995

"What d'ya mean you got a problem with Mr de Klerk?" asked the policeman, quickly becoming hostile, swelling his chest amid the newly beefed up security of the Union Buildings' east wing.

"No, not a problem, an appointment."

"Oh."

But it was too late. The die was cast. The opinion formed. I was an instant security risk and gaining entry to the office of South Africa's deputy president - easily achieved only a week before - was to be a trial of endurance and humility.

Still, after the tales of Al Gore's henchmen pushing local dignitaries up against the wall, it was a cinch.

And, in the gloom of his expansive office, South Africa's deputy president was at relative ease in a snappy blue silk shirt.

"I thought you were meant to be on holiday," I say.

"I am," he replies, adding he had been visiting his sick mother down the road.

It is ironic that February 2 1990, day zero, is beginning to feel like an albatross to FW de Klerk - at least that's the impression one gets.

Not that he regrets what happened then or has happened since. Far from it. It's just that the past has a magnetism that seems to constantly draw the attention back, reminding one of the pain and the anguish of our infamous history. And perhaps of the NP's role in that history.

"The further we move away from 1990, which was really when everything began, the more we need to concentrate on the future and on the challenges which lie ahead," he says.

"Too much energy has been spent on recriminations and on shifting blame."

The energy spent on recrimination was such that, in January this year, the NP seriously considered leaving the government of national unity.

The crisis occurred in the wake of the discovery by Dullah Omar, the minister of justice, that 3,500 former security force officials - including Adriaan Vlok, the former minister of law and order, and Magnus Malan, the former minister of defence - had applied for automatic indemnity for crimes committed during the apartheid era.

In the ensuing brouhaha, harsh words were exchanged between Mandela and De Klerk in which the integrity of both men were questioned.

But, following the decision of the two leaders to make a fresh start, it was time that thoughts of splitting the government were entertained by the NP.

The row brought into sharp relief the need for clearly defining the interaction and role of the parties within the forced coalition that is the government of national unity.

The NP began to thrash out exactly how it could combine its dual role as both opposition and ally, challenger, and partner. "There is room for differences as well as the need for the two parties to maintain a clear-cut profile."

The parties agreed that firm guidelines were needed to govern interparty relations to prevent the development of an equally serious crisis in the future, or worse. At the next cabinet *bosberaad*, which will be held early in the New Year, these guidelines are expected to be completed and approved.

"We need to find a way to work together." In the meantime, "we are achieving a rhythm in that regard."

But the spectre of apartheid era crimes and indemnity applications continue to haunt the political landscape. The murder trial of Malan and 19 other security force officials and the impending truth commission are testimony to continuing currency of the past.

"We will continue to press for evenhandedness," De Klerk says of his party's attitude. Situations comparable to human rights abuses alleged in the Malan trial, which members of the ANC leadership were involved, should be dealt with in exactly the same way.

The granting of temporary immunity to some ANC leaders require revision to ensure this, he says.

It is obvious that while acknowledging the necessity and value of determining the truth, De Klerk would much rather move away from the ugliness and bitterness of the past.

"We need to spend much more energy in developing the policy frameworks, and then implementing them, which can bring prosperity and stability for all the people of South Africa."

While 1994 was a year for settling down in the new dispensation, this year has been a year of adaptation, according to De Klerk.

The high points include positive economic developments, growing international and domestic confidence and the appearance of the first fruits of the reconstruction and development programme.

The RDP has taken too long to get going and is still lagging in some areas, he says. "But things are coming together and moving forward to a situation where the RDP can be expected to yield results."

As far as next year is concerned, our priorities can be singled out: law and order, the constitution, the economy, and the RDP.

A clampdown on crime, and on violent crime in particular, is an urgent requirement, De Klerk says.

The absence of the Inkatha Freedom Party is a major stumbling block to the successful completion of the constitutional process. While it is technically possible to pass the new constitution without the participation of the IFP, "whether that is advisable or not is another question. We would be drifting into the same situation as before the election."

While welcoming the tone of the recent meeting between Mandela and the IFP leader, Mangosuthu Buthelezi, De Klerk is calling on the ANC to pursue "a continued and intensified political initiative" to ensure that the IFP returns to the constitutional assembly.

The maintenance and intensification of South Africa's economic momentum and implementation of the RDP are also critical objectives of the year ahead.

But at the heart of South Africa's growth and transition is the need for the reassertion of moral values and fibre, De Klerk argues. A highly competitive world demands that South Africa should shine in all field of activity, maintaining high standards where they exist and working hard to establish them where they do not.

"Only if we excel in what we do will we be able to compete successfully to the benefit of all our people."

12 KWAZULU-NATAL: 'WILL THERE BE ANYONE LEFT TO BURY US?'

January 21 1996

Elizabeth Cele does not know who burst into her kraal last month and slaughtered five members of her family. She does not know who, and she does not know why.

It was dark, she says, and late. Everyone was asleep. She thinks perhaps politics was to blame as she lives in an area of KwaZulu-Natal's south coast considered to be an Inkatha Freedom Party stronghold, but it is possible some grievance or grudge was being evened up with one of her family members.

All Elizabeth knows for sure is that on December 15 last year, half her family was shot to death.

"We are sick of burying people," the Reverend Danny Chetty, who operates Practical Ministeries, a church-based relief agency in the area, said recently in an open letter to President Nelson Mandela

"As the killing continues, and even escalates, we are beginning to wonder whether, when our turn comes, there will be anybody left to bury us."

Within 10 days of the Cele family murder last month, two more massacres had taken place in the rural hinterland not far from the south coast resort town of Port Shepstone. In the third attack, at Shobashobane, on Christmas Day, 19 people were killed and dozens injured in an operation of almost military proportions.

Estimates vary of how many have died in the cycle of violence that has wracked KwaZulu-Natal for 10 years. Hopes that the election of a government of national unity would somehow still the killing fields have proved to be in vain.

The human rights committee said that 835 political deaths were recorded in the province during 1995, along with many more hurt and left homeless. The focus of much of this violence has been in a small pocket of territory wedged between the northern Eastern Cape border running past Kokstad and the strip of resorts and timeshares falling south of Durban along the Indian Ocean.

Deeply rural, the area these days has all the trappings of a war zone. At night, a security force helicopter clatters into the silence; its powerful spotlight flitting and pausing on ravines, cane fields and kraals.

Below, returning refugees huddle together in army tents near the burnt-out shells of their homes and silent graves of their families and friends. Armoured vehicles patrol along roads muddied by summer rains.

Almost without exception, people from the area blame politics for the deaths and disruption. But, on closer questioning, the many different conceptions of what politics actually means throws light on just how complex the issues are and how difficult it is going to be to resolve them.

"It's fundamentally a political power struggle between the youth, who began to be mobilised in the late 1980s, and the conservative tribal and familial structures," says a former school principal who was forced to flee the violence.

The former principal, whose Baboyi school fell on the dividing line between an ANC and an IFP area, says the clash between generations is fuelled by a lack of political education and intolerance. "We lost some of our most promising students in the violence while the school itself was often in the crossfire."

The main cause is the political conflict between the IFP and the ANC, which began in the area during the days of the United Democratic Front and accelerated once the ANC was unbanned in 1990, says Winston Mavundla, a local traditional leader.

For him, politics is a power struggle between the leaderships of the two parties, a struggle exacerbated by dishonesty and motivated by the quest for status, followers, and territory.

“When the (leaders) speak they do not speak with one language. During the day, a person wears a sheepskin but at night a jackal skin. This is confusing the people. Political leaders have to sit down and speak in real terms, not bluff each other”.

It is most definitely political, says the head of the special police investigation unit appointed to look into the December massacres, director Bushie Engelbrecht. But while political power may be the central objective, a criminal element has also begun to creep into the equation. “I wonder whether certain people aren’t misusing the situation to enrich themselves,” Engelbrecht muses.

Meanwhile, the mayor of neighbouring Port Shepstone, Pauline Duncan, says the violence has been happening year after year and is a historical thing between the ANC and IFP “going back to the days of tribal revenge and avenge”.

Describing herself as “non-party political”, Duncan agrees that the example for political tolerance and cooperation has to come from the top, from the leadership.

“Make clear the violence is not happening in Port Shepstone,” she says. “All the violence is out of town, in Izingolweni. That’s not our area.”

Bruce Walker, the local peace committee co-ordinator, argues that the violence will continue as long as the national constitutional impasse remains, and traditional leaders fail to reconcile differences and set an example.

The breakdown of the judicial and policing system in the province and the failure of the security forces to apprehend, prosecute and punish the perpetrators of the violence are additional and important elements.

This, says Walker, is further spurred by high rates of unemployment and the resultant frustration among the youth, boredom, idleness, ubiquitous crime and a lack of education concerning political tolerance, together with allegations of security force complicity in some attacks.

Phansi Cele, who claims to be 95, is one of the survivors of the Shobashabane massacre. Early on Christmas morning he had been drinking beer with friends when he heard the shots in the distance.

The reason for the attack was "just to kill the ANC," he says.

"They told us to go away from here, that they didn't want the ANC here, that this place was for the IFP. Then they burnt houses and shot people."

Local IFP leader Themba Mtuli says the violence is caused by the ANC bringing its supporters from the urban areas and settling them in the rural parts of southern KwaZulu-Natal.

The ANC does not accept that the IFP won the province in the last election and is determined to make it ungovernable, he says.

"The ANC strategy is that if it sees it has no support in an area, it will bring people in from urban areas."

Mtuli says ANC supporters have scant respect for tribal structures, and provincial and national leaders become too involved in local issues and problems.

Regional chairperson of the ANC in the lower south coast area, Ravi Pillay, argues that the highs and lows of violence correspond to "what is on the political agenda at any time".

"The dilemma we face is that we have a responsibility to the party to build it and that in many areas members want to get organised. But if we go there, set up an interim committee, distribute pamphlets and hold a small meeting, it's guaranteed within 48 hours someone will be dead."

The IFP, says Pillay, is not prepared to tolerate an ANC presence in most rural areas. "It's the thin edge of the wedge."

He argues that a hard-core controlling faction within the IFP has placed the parties on a collision course of conflict and that tolerance and development are vital ingredients in any bid to quell the violence.

The disarming of the population, together with visible and effective policing, are also critical.

The causes of the violence, then, in the southern coastal region of KwaZulu-Natal are varied and complex.

According to the people most directly affected, the continuing deaths are about a frail judicial and enforcement system battling to assert neutrality and efficiency. They are about a national constitutional impasse and a lack of genuine will from political leaders - national, provincial, and local - to merge traditional systems of leadership with democracy and tolerance.

The murders are about underlying socio-economic conditions of poverty, unemployment and a lack of resources and development. And they are about the age-old tensions between city and countryside, and between youth and their elders.

For each of those approached, from massacre survivor to police officer, from peace worker to schoolteacher, politics is the catch-all, the scourge and the cause of the loss of life. But for every one, the notion of politics contains a different meaning, with truth in each.

Any bid to solve the problem of violence will have to address the many truths.

13 DESMOND TUTU: 'IF WE DON'T HEAL, WE ARE GOING TO DESTROY'

February 18 1996

Archbishop Desmond Mpilo Tutu is sitting under a tree at the bottom of his garden, reading aloud to a small group of children at his feet.

It is a spitefully hot summer afternoon in Cape Town, still and humid, especially in a thick purple archbishop's cassock.

Tutu is getting irritated.

"I thought you said five minutes," he says, pausing his rendition of Cinderella. "This is the longest five minutes of my life".

"We're almost there," says the photographer.

"One, two, three, four, five," Tutu reads, quite loud now, drawing the children's attention to him once more. Ever patient. Mollified, briefly, by their beatific smiles.

"Pull it down a bit," the photographer says to one of his assistants, who is hanging from a branch nearby, drawing it down.

"I think he's getting annoyed," one of Tutu's aids says. "He'll be off *Cinderella* and on to *Snow White* just now."

Suddenly, it's over. The photo shoot is finished. Another appointment complete. The children scatter. The photographic team begins to pack earnestly. The archbishop's aides sigh.

Tutu marches back up the lawn, back into the cool sanctity of his study and into a cotton shirt more appropriate to the sticky Cape heat.

But, just as he is about to enter the French doors of Bishopscourt, the archbishop's residence, he turns and pauses. Table Mountain, its slopes and features are perfectly clear. The sky is a deep, African blue. Cloudless. Pink rhododendrons line the driveway. A fountain spatters in the centre of the brick courtyard.

"I'm going to miss this place," he says ruefully.

After almost 10 years, another phase in the famous life of Desmond Tutu is drawing to an end.

He is now only "nominally" archbishop. A vicar general has been appointed to oversee the diocese until his successor has been elected. Tutu will relinquish his position on June 3 this year.

His tenure as archbishop has embraced an astonishing period in South African history, perhaps its most astonishing.

"When I came here, in September 1986, it was at the height of one state of emergency or another. It comes as something of a shock to realise I've been here that long," he says. "It was a very rough time for many people, but not that much for me."

He recalls various set-tos with the then State President, PW Botha, the vilification he suffered at the hands of the South African Broadcasting Corporation and the baboon foetuses that were hammered to the trees at Bishopscourt to intimidate him.

"For many white people I was the person they most loved to hate. Even travelling on domestic flights then was a very unpleasant experience; you could have cut the atmosphere with a knife when I walked on to the plane. If looks could kill, we would have been murdered many times."

Just as the churches took the helm of the internal liberation struggle, so Bishopscourt became a sanctuary in those hard years.

"Justice will prevail, we told ourselves, despite all appearances to the contrary; don't worry, it'll be all right."

It is little wonder that President Nelson Mandela went to Bishopscourt as soon as he was released from prison in 1990. It was here that he spent his first night of real freedom and it was under these trees that he gave his first press conference.

"It has been an incredible vindication, a wonderful cherry on the treetop. Justice *will* prevail. God has been very generous."

Tutu had three goals when he was first elected as archbishop: the liberation of South Africa's people, the ordination of women and the division of the diocese.

"The first two have been achieved and the third looks likely. But even two out of three is a fairly high [success] rate."

One of the perks of being the archbishop of Cape Town is the automatic assumption of the title of vice president of the Western Province Cricket Club. But, like the formal openings of Parliament to which he was always invited, he never made use of the opportunity.

"Now, after democracy, I have been to the opening of Parliament twice, including when President Mandela was elected, and I was at Newlands cricket ground when we beat England so thoroughly.

"When I see Parliament now, I think it's not true, that it's just a dream, a dream of what things could be; the woman speaker, all the black faces, the president. It just looks so normal, how it is. It's incredible."

Several months ago, Tutu had planned to retire. He had accepted a visiting professorship at a university in Atlanta, Georgia, in the United States, and was going to teach and write a book.

"I was hoping to slip out quietly into a more reflective lifestyle."

Coincidentally, the Tutus would have arrived in Atlanta just before this year's Olympic Games and he and his wife, Leah, both avid sports fans, were looking forward to it.

But his God has not finished with Desmond Tutu. Perhaps his most important chapter, his most difficult challenge and maybe even his greatest triumph, is yet to come.

Rather than ministering to a suffering nation, he was called, at the age of 64, to help heal it by leading the truth commission.

"It's a very deeply, very profoundly spiritual engagement," he told a packed press conference earlier in the week. "If it succeeds in its work, the repercussions for South Africa will be very considerable. If it fails, as someone once said: the consequences will be too ghastly to contemplate."

Tutu is all too aware that the 17 members of the commission will be under enormous pressure to act impartially, independently and fairly over the 18-month lifespan of the body. He is also aware that the legislation is a middle way, a negotiated compromise, which doesn't even require the perpetrators of gross human rights violations to say they are sorry.

"There are those who would opt for amnesia and those who want retribution and revenge. The commission is a settlement between the two compromises."

He is sceptical about the chances of the commission leading to vengeance or to injustice: "People know they've been victims and often who did it. The families know. The Mxenges know. The Bikos know. They have known for years but they haven't used the knowledge as a means of goading themselves or others into an orgy of revenge.

"Frank Chikane knows who his torturer was; he has even met him. I'm not aware that he has gone around whipping up emotions and calling for revenge. But it's very difficult to give anyone assurances until we're able to demonstrate what we're about.

"Also it would be very difficult, as someone who has fought for justice for all those years, to find myself now involved in injustice. If we don't heal we are going to destroy. I myself believe we will heal."

In the meantime, there are more meetings and appointments to attend to. "I'm so busy I hardly have time to breathe," he chuckles.

Around him are the artefacts of a monumental life: human-rights awards and correspondence from the Nobel foundation, family portraits, a signed poster from Bill Cosby, a gleaming steel crucifix.

Maybe when the next Olympic Games comes round, he will have a little more time to enjoy them.

14 MANGOSUTHU BUTHELEZI: 'NOT YET UHURU'

February 25 1996.

It's the first time it's rained in Cape Town for weeks; a thin drizzle that hovers in drifts over the city. It's early evening but the thin Eid moon is hidden by a twilight mist.

Eight floors up, in the slim Plein Street office block housing most of the government of national unity's ministries, the home affairs minister and Inkatha Freedom Party leader, Mangosuthu Buthelezi, settles into a comfortable armchair in his office.

He is fidgety but seems relatively at ease, often closing his eyes while speaking. "I wouldn't say I was happy," he says, reflecting on his position in the constellation that is South Africa's current political setup.

"South Africans in a sense are in a fool's paradise. It's never worked throughout history that a majority tramples on a minority, or a minority tramples on a majority. While I rejoice in having a black president, South Africa has not yet reached its destination ... it's not yet Uhuru."

He laments in particular what he sees as the shoddy treatment of the IFP in all realms of government, from diplomatic appointments and constitutional negotiations to cabinet meetings. His suggestions and arguments are ignored in the cabinet, he says, or quickly quashed with a simple majority vote.

"On many occasions I have objected not only verbally but in writing. But they say 'please note what the minister of home affairs has said' and move on.

There have been no IFP ambassadors appointed and the ANC's steadfast refusal to entertain the notion of international mediation has kept the party out of the constitutional assembly since February last year.

"If I had known the president was deceiving me [on the mediation issue], I would not have gone to the [April 1994] elections."

He is resigned, it seems, to his party playing no further part in drawing up the new national constitution. While the IFP has been able to make some contributions, such as the double-ballot voting system used in 1994 and the drive for provincial autonomy, this has been inadequate.

How stable will the country be with a contested constitution; Buthelezi wouldn't like to guess. "I never indulge in visions or say what is going to happen."

But it is to his apparently worsening relationship with President Nelson Mandela that he keeps returning. He seems bitter and feels Mandela has snubbed and mistreated him, despite their public affability.

"Madiba is a hero to all of us, a martyr, a saint, an icon. But because of this aura it allows him to do things, and no one will criticise him. But things are not really right."

He talks of broken promises and lapsed agreements, of wishful intentions and unfulfilled engagements.

"Now that he [Mandela] is at the helm and things are going well no-one wants to upset the applecart ... but I cannot understand his intransigence."

Buthelezi is a self-confessed workaholic and spends long hours at the office, often until midnight and beyond. "Mine is usually the last car to leave," he says.

He has a plaster on his little finger, injured by a canvas strip during the constant packing and unpacking every cabinet minister and many civil servants must endure.

On the pending resumption of the murder trial of former minister of defence Magnus Malan together with the IFP's deputy secretary-general MZ Khumalo, and others, Buthelezi says: "People forget there was a people's war. The order to kill all collaborators is well documented."

"I never ran any hit squads and not a single person has been killed on my orders."

At the time 200 IFP members went for military training in the Caprivi Strip in the mid-1980s, "I had a small police force, but it wasn't adequate or big enough. We had received threats that hit squads would be coming to Ulundi to blow up buildings, and we thought that we needed assistance."

He confirms that the Truth and Reconciliation Commission's chairman, Archbishop Desmond Tutu, and its deputy chairman, Alex Boraine, have requested a meeting. He will probably accede but feels he has nothing to say to the commission.

A number of other issues continue to irritate him: the apparent anti-IFP bias of the special police investigation teams in KwaZulu-Natal, and the amendment of the Ingonyama Trust Act and the implications of this for central government interference in provincial affairs.

But there is much in his own portfolio to keep him busy. As one ministerial secretary was overheard saying: "Every day somebody dies, every day somebody is born, every day somebody leaves the country, every day somebody comes in, every weekend someone gets married: all these people come to home affairs. I'm going to take early retirement."

Then there is an election to prepare for, of course. Up on the eighth floor, there's a light shining in the late evening gloom.

15 NELSON MANDELA'S DIVORCE HEARING

March 24, 1996

(Nelson and Winnie Mandela were married in June 1958. Nelson was imprisoned for life in 1964 having spent several years either on trial or on the run evading police capture. Winnie was banished to a small village and saw little of Nelson for the 27 years he was in prison. Nelson and Winnie spent some time together after his release from prison in 1990 but separated in 1992. Though mired in controversy, Winnie was appointed to the cabinet in 1994 in Nelson's Government of National Unity as deputy minister of arts, culture, science and technology. She was fired after 11 months by Nelson for fraud and unauthorised absences. They finalised their divorce in March 1996).

The courtroom is no strange place for Nelson Mandela. Over the years, key moments not only in his life but also in the life of the nation have been played out before the thin wood veneers, flickering strip lighting, black gowns and broken clocks that still adorn the halls of justice.

But it is almost 32 years since the Black Pimpernel, then outlaw and revolutionary, was last in the witness box. His performances then and now have always been compelling.

"I feel oppressed by the atmosphere of white domination that lurks all around in this courtroom," he announced while conducting his own defence in the famous treason trial of 1960.

He called on the judge to recuse himself, questioned the very nature of the justice system and pilloried hapless witnesses - particularly those from the security branch.

Yet even as he railed against the system, explained the genesis and objectives of the ANC and of Umkhonto weSizwe, a hint of the personal cost of his endeavours invariably found their way into the proceedings.

It was a plaintive cry, buried among the volume and significance of more weighty matters, but it is one worth recalling: "It has not been easy for me during the past period to separate myself from my wife and children," he told those present at the Old Synagogue Court in Pretoria in 1962.

"To say goodbye to the good old days when, at the end of a strenuous day at an office, I could look forward to joining my family at the dinner table and instead to take up the life of a man hunted continuously by the police, living separated from those who are closest to me, in my own country, facing continually the hazards of detection and of arrest.

"This has been a life infinitely more difficult than serving a prison sentence. But there comes a time when a man is denied the right to live a normal life, when he can only live the life of an outlaw because the government has so decreed to use the law to impose a state of outlawry upon him. I was driven to this situation, and I do not regret having taken the decisions that I did take."

And so history staked its claim to the life of Nelson Mandela. And 32 years later he again climbed into the witness box.

The courtroom this time was populated by a very different group of people, far closer to representing the nation's diversity than in the early 1960s.

He was in a lightly striped charcoal pinstripe and wore, for a few brief moments, a half-smile.

"Yes, Wim, how are you?" he addressed his counsel, Wim Trengove SC. Mandela's expression gradually became a smile as he put on his glasses and began to read through the documents before him.

He occasionally looked about, nodding at familiar faces. Every now and then he took off his glasses, rested his chin on one hand, and just stared ahead. He often seemed twisted in his chair.

Winnie entered in a rush of activity, about five or ten minutes late. She avoided looking at him for a while then peeked down the table, past Trengove, to where Mandela was looking through the documents. He wasn't looking, so she turned away. Mandela then stole a glance, but again they missed each other. Later, after he had finished being cross-examined, he went over, shook the hands of Winnie's counsel, then hers, but still he avoided looking into her eyes.

It was a painful, difficult business.

Winnie Madikizela-Mandela fired her counsel in a bid to secure a postponement, saying "I am just an ordinary person, I am not equipped to put witnesses in the box on my behalf and then question them. There is nothing I can do on my own. I am just an ordinary person."

In the box, Mandela was succinct but generous in his portrayal of Winnie.

But he would not allow any over-eulogising by Winnie's counsel Ismail Semenya.

"She was part of a collective. None of us can be described as having virtues or qualities that raise him or her above others. There are many women in this country who suffered far more than she did."

At times, he threatened Semenya not to push him: "I appeal to you, do not ask me questions which might compel me to damage the image of the defendant [Winnie] and which will cause pain to our children and grandchildren."

It was a masterly, though genuine performance that not only fascinated the world but made history too.

There's simply no holding down a man of destiny.

In his darkest and most humiliating hour, he exudes dignity and forbearance. In circumstances of tawdry self-revelation, he drums up pathos and admiration. In the most menial of situations, he creates precedents that will survive for generations.

In reporting the details of the case, whole swathes of the divorce act were cast out the window, one media lawyer said this week.

What happened in the court this week could have a whole range of implications, including constitutional.

According to the lawyer it is open season on any public figure involved in a divorce case, especially as the presiding officer in the landmark case was Judge President Frikkie Eloff.

Other precedents set during the Mandela trial this week include what is probably the first time that a South African judge has presided over a divorce hearing.

It is also virtually unheard of for a current head of state to enter the witness box to reveal the details of his personal life.

Mandela did not want to appear in court or have his dirty laundry inspected. The way in which he was made to do this was cruel and unnecessary.

However, Mandela's adherence to transparency and to the right of the public to know is once more testimony to a man who has been destined always to wear his life, and his heart, on his sleeve.

16 LOOKING BACK ON THE FIRST TWO YEARS OF DEMOCRACY

April 28 1996

In the beginning, there were the queues. Great long ones, three, sometimes four people wide, curling around buildings and down streets, circling car parks and crossing dusty schoolyards.

Served by food vendors, crowned by umbrellas, and infused with limitless patience and a grim collective determination, they heralded in a new era in South Africa. An era of choice and of democracy. An era of reconstruction. The Mandela era.

Election day. April 27 1994.

It's two years ago now, almost to the day, since South Africans voted together for the first time.

In two years, it's easy to forget the atmosphere of fear and violence and the dire warnings of social and political strife that characterised the build-up to that famous poll[3]; the pre-election bombing campaign by the rightwing that killed and maimed people across the country (and for which life sentences were handed down only recently); the Shell House carnage when Inkatha impis marched from Soweto into central Johannesburg, turning the city into a bloody

---

[3] See the Timetable in the front of this book and also the Preface for more details on this dangerous period.

battleground.

The East Rand, heart of the nation's manufacturing and industrial sector, was a war zone, torn apart by political faction fighting between hostel dwellers and township residents, and exacerbated by the efforts of the hastily established and ill-prepared national peacekeeping force.

Politically and infrastructurally, the election seemed a haphazard roll of the dice at best. At worst, a certain invitation to conflagration and civil war.

Little wonder that the supermarkets were deluged with anxious patrons eager to stock up with siege rations of baked beans and candles while others sought refuge in faraway cities.

Nowhere did the endeavour appear more risky than in KwaZulu-Natal. Political violence continued to take the lives of people in the province every week. The vast distance, rural topography and huge number of people complicated the already difficult logistics of voter education and of the actual voting process.

Scepticism over the province's level of preparedness, together with a suspicion of the major parties' intentions, meant the IFP leader Mangosuthu Buthelezi, refused to bring his party into the poll until only a few weeks before.

Unable to make use of the discredited and potentially partial department of home affairs in its standard role of election planner and co-ordinator, the temporary multiparty governing body, the Transitional Executive Council, created the Independent Electoral Commission to oversee the poll.

It was only later, when the IEC's records had been audited, that it was realised just how inefficient and profligate that body had been. Only a special tax, the transitional levy, could recover the hundreds of millions of rands that fed the IEC.

Remember the millions of ballot papers being flown in by jumbo from London - needlessly as it turned out. Remember the striking counters and officials, the inadequate distribution of ballot boxes, papers and ultraviolet lights. Remember the mayhem during the staggered announcement of results at Gallagher Estate in Midrand.

It seemed incredible then, and it seems incredible now, that the election took place, let alone in a manner that was free and fair.

But, somehow, the inevitable march of history and the ineluctable logic of democracy were not to be denied or forestalled.

The inauguration itself, as the flight of fighter jets trailed smoke over the Union Buildings, seemed proof enough that the nation and the world believed in the miracle of the rainbow nation.

In retrospect, the 1994 election taught South Africa much about itself and about the new global community in which it found itself.

Caught up in post-election fervour, who doubted the necessity and vision of the Reconstruction and Development Programme? It was on everybody's lips for months. Hardly a company was without its proudly announced contribution to the RDP, hardly a new product or project without an RDP slant or spinoff.

While political parties fought for ownership of the process, and the public laboured under the new concepts and language of RDP-speak, criticism was scoffed at and deemed unpatriotic, unprogressive or even racist.

And yet, with hindsight, the RDP was chimera. Laudable, moral, even essential in its intention, but the emperor had no clothes. For two years the signs of feeble RDP delivery went unheeded. Who would have believed then, in those heady days, how the RDP would soon lie, disbanded and all but forgotten?

We may be a determined, gritty lot, but we certainly can be naive.

We soon realised, too, that all those offers of help and assistance made during the presidential inauguration arrived with more string than wrapping paper. The quickly liberalising world markets would also soon provide a tough challenge to South African economic and foreign policy.

We acquired a taste, too, for the politics of brinkmanship during those days. No problem was too tractable, no crisis too mild to solve at the very last moment.

Little wonder the new constitution is going to be finalised at the stroke of midnight or that forthcoming local elections in KwaZulu-Natal still hang in the balance.

It was inevitable, too, that the 1994 election would have a huge impact on the structure of politics and of political parties in South Africa.

The ANC emerged, as expected, with a landslide national victory and established itself as the dominant political force in the country.

The election signalled the rise of the Freedom Front, the fall of the Pan Africanist Congress and the entrenchment of the IFP as a force to be reckoned with in KwaZulu-Natal.

The National Party is still struggling to come to terms with its past and establish a platform for the future, while the Democratic Party hovers at the margins.

The election also saw the demise of extra-parliamentary politics and the creation, still in its infancy, of provincially based centres of power.

But perhaps the most noteworthy development of the past two years has been the ascendancy of President Nelson Mandela to almost mythic proportions. While this has undoubtedly been good for national unity and reconciliation, his huge domestic and international status has its downside too. At the merest hint of ill-health, investment dries up, the market panics and the rand plummets to new lows.

While Deputy President Thabo Mbeki is very much Mandela's heir apparent, particularly after ANC secretary general Cyril Ramaphosa's announced move to the private sector, the fear of life after Mandela continues to haunt the political and economic landscape.

Two years on, while crime, poverty, unemployment, and homelessness still befuddle policy planners, who would now question the process that brought South Africans to the polls together for the first time? It was an election that ushered in a new era. There will never be another one quite like it.

17 PATRICIA DE LILLE: 'I DON'T FEEL PART OF THINGS'

March 14 1999

Not long after being sworn in as an MP for the Pan Africanist Congress, Patricia de Lille heard a knock at the door.

Standing there was as a senior policeman, Captain Markus-Antonius Jonker, the acting commissioner of the Steenberg police station.

"I am here because you are really my last hope," he told De Lille. "Please help me."

During the latter years of the struggle, the PAC had developed a reputation not only for killing white people in general - the St James church massacre and the Heidelberg Tavern incidents being examples - but for killing policemen in particular.

After the initial surprise, De Lille took in Jonker, listened to his problems, and agreed to do what she could. "I went out here to the community and helped him out," she says now.

Jonker won his private battle and staved off the transfer he had been so desperate to avoid.

The anecdote says much about De Lille and about the PAC too. "All of us have baggage and we have tried very hard to speak out of that mould. But people prefer to remember us as the party who thought up 'one settler, one bullet'.

The Jonker case, though, is far from a lonely example. De Lille's life is littered with such interventions. On our way into parliament's gardens to take some pictures, a parliamentary service officer called out "Thanks very much, Patricia. I'll come and see you again when I'm 70."

The man, it turned out, had been threatened with forced retirement because he was 65 years old. Together, he and De Lille sought out several other senior service officers at a more advanced age and argued that they should also be retired. The man kept his job.

Back in the office, the phone rings. It seems that earlier in the week, De Lille had led a delegation of 800 people to the town council offices of Calitzdorp in the Karoo. She had forced her way into a council meeting to ask why members of the community had been charged up to R500 for water when their meters were buried under several feet of sand and hadn't been looked at for years.

Threatening to sue the council for fraud, De Lille extracted one concession after another from them. Each time she secured a concession, she went outside to address the 800 people and each time they cheered. Inside, when things got tough, she told the council "look at the people outside, they elected you and they are angry".

By the end of it, the PAC had three new councillors, the community had won a string of agreements - including two tarred roads - and a thousand PAC membership forms had been snapped up with another thousand on the way.

De Lille was born and raised in Beaufort West and still misses its wide-open spaces and the clear skies of the Karoo. "It took me a long time to adapt to city life," she says.

She went straight into work after school at a Plascon paint factory. With her father, a teacher, being the only breadwinner and her brother studying pharmacy at the University of Cape Town, the family needed the money.

To write her final school exams, De Lille needed an identity book. In her book, her race was described as “mixed”.

“I was very, very angry. I couldn’t accept that other human beings had the right to say we weren’t South Africans and to tag us in that way. My father used to say there was only one race and that was the human race. We were never allowed to speak in terms of black or white in the house. But outside, I was conscious of the contradictions.

As with others, the uprising of June 1976 was a formative moment for De Lille. She decided she must contribute in some way to the fight against apartheid. However she did not have a political home. “I looked at the documents from all the parties: the Freedom Charter, the Cape Action League’s 10-point plan, Azapo, the New Unity Movement - and they weren’t easy to get hold of because all the documents were banned. The PAC was the only party that actually said that instead of describing their members as being from this or that race, they gave a definition of an African. ‘Here is a definition of an African,’ it said, ‘if you accept this, you are an African.’

“That gave me a sense of belonging. I had been born and bred in Africa and had been denied being part of Africa. I have always had an obsession with identity and have never accepted that one must be identified according to the old Population Registration Act.”

Signing up with the PAC was not an easy task, given the 1976 uprising and the party’s banning. In the workplace, De Lille had become involved in the South African Chemical Workers’ Union and went on to become deputy president of the National Council of Trade Unions (NCTU).

As a senior unionist, she began to travel. In Gaborone, Botswana, she approached the late Elizabeth Sibeko, a PAC representative, and asked to join.

"She was very suspicious. In exile you didn't know who to trust. There was a lot of infiltration and if they didn't know you, they were very wary of you."

After a week-long conference, she had made the grade and, back home, was introduced to the other members of a local PAC cell. When the party was unbanned in 1990, De Lille took up a full-time job to build the NCTU in the Western Cape.

"We completely underestimated the elections in 1994," she says. "We packaged and marketed our message wrongly. We thought that if the message was good enough - and it was beautiful message - that we didn't need to worry about infrastructure to sustain the message and compete with other parties. We finally learned that 98 percent of the campaign is organising, co-ordinating and managing and only 2 percent is the message."

Only a handful of PAC members made it to parliament and De Lille was one of them. Five years later, the experience has been a difficult one but not one De Lille regrets. "I had always hated this institution and then I became part of it, part of a system I had been fighting against my whole life. It was difficult for me to change.

"We came here without understanding the processes involved. We didn't know we first had to tell people we needed to change the laws.

"We were all a bit naive. The method of struggle had changed. We couldn't get anywhere by jumping up and down, demanding this or that. We needed information, statistics, to make a valuable input. Rhetoric didn't work."

Being part of the opposition has also had its frustrations.

"The ANC treats the opposition parties as if they are all the same. But we are quite different from the traditional white parties, the DP and the NP, who want to retain as much of the the status quo as possible.

"On some issues the PAC is in agreement with the ANC and its objectives. It's on how to achieve these that we differ.

"The sad part is that there is no acknowledgement from the ANC and that is one of our major frustrations.

"I go into the national assembly to speak. I've done the research. I've spoken to people. I really feel I can make a contribution, suggest some proposals. But I'm just ignored ... I feel like I'm speaking for the sake of Hansard and for the media to report. I don't really feel part of things."

The ANC, De Lille says, has become increasingly arrogant over the past five years.

"They alone know that is best for this country, they have no need to listen. They are power-drunk and that is where they've made their mistake.

"They have a monopoly on policy that has caused a gap to slowly widen between us and the people out there.

"I find the same people are making policy as in the past. Millions of rands are spent on consultants who produce glossy documents. And once it is in the glossy documents, even if it's not working, they follow blindly and make mistakes.

"I hope that in the next parliament the policy process will bring in the people that matter. Those millions should be used for improving the capacity of the historically disadvantaged to contribute to policymaking. I've always thought that personal experience is the best teacher."

18 SELBY BAQWA TRIES HIS HAND AT BEING A THEATRE CRITIC

June 8 1996

(In 1995, a new position was created in South Africa, that of Public Protector. The post was intended to be an ombudsman-type position charged with supporting and defending democracy by, among other things, investigating corruption and fraud within government. Selby Baqwa, a lawyer and judge, was the inaugural appointment. One of his first major tasks was to investigate the commissioning of a play about HIV-Aids, Sarafina 2, by a government department at the exorbitant cost of SAR14,2-million [+/-£2-million])

Many are the functions and broad is the ambit of South Africa's first Public Protector, Selby Baqwa.

According to the Public Protector Act 23 of 1994, he is entitled to investigate not only maladministration, corruption and prejudice at all levels of government, but also "capricious, discourteous or other improper conduct".

But nowhere in the law, nowhere in the Constitution and nowhere in the selection interviews was it mentioned to Baqwa that one of his first challenges was to be a theatre critic.

And yet, in his very first case, this is exactly the thespian art to which he was required to turn his critical eye.

In section 7.4 of his already famous report on *Sarafina 2*, our public protector gets right down to the scene of the crime and, notebook in hand, begins to pen a critique of the work.

"The play has some excellent music and dance routines," he reports, "and is quite entertaining". But, he continues later, "for the department to justify spending R14,2-million, one would have expected so much more."

Quite. But, short of a fireworks display you could see from Bloemfontein, a cast of thousands and guest appearances by Demi Moore and Arnold

Schwarzenegger, I doubt there was ever even the faintest likelihood of such criteria being met. More to the point, our public protector surely has more appropriate duties with which to concern himself.

It is not *Sarafina 2* being a bad play that is the issue.

In any case, these things are subjective, to say the least.

We all have opinions, often differing, on the performing arts and on the manner in which these arts are performed.

In fact, Baqwa was warned of this by certain wise officials. "During the hearings, officials of the (health) department conveyed to me that there can never be total agreement among experts on what messages should be conveyed. This could be so but I have little doubt the present product can be improved on."

Some express their opinions on the arts better than others.

While it would be a disservice to both to enter into a serious comparison, few were better at the fine art of slagging off a bad play than Dorothy Parker.

"It was a dull, silly, dirty play," she wrote following the premiere of *Lady Beyond the Moon* in the New Yorker in 1931.

In another classic, concerning the play *Right of Happiness*, she said: "It is so truly abominally written and devised that it would have been ridiculous had it not been so stultifyingly a bore".

One of Parker's best put downs, however, concerned a play by AA Milne, *Give Me Yesterday*, which featured a particularly close moment between a cabinet minister - no relation - and his boyhood love.

The two had communicated in years long gone by tapping out letters of the alphabet on their shared wall: one tap for an "a", two for a "b" , and so on.

Here is Parker at her best: "The cabinet minister talks softly and embarrassingly to Sally - Ah, Selly, Selly, Selly' - but that is not enough. He must tap out to her, on the garden wall, his message, though she is right beside him. First he taps, and at the length it would take, the "I". Then he goes into "l", and though everyone in the audience has caught the idea, he carries through to "o".

"Oh, he's not going on to "v", I said to myself. Even Milne wouldn't do that to you. But he did. He tapped on through "v", and then did an "e". If he does 'y', I thought, I'm through. And he did. So I shot myself.

"It was, unhappily, a nothing - oh, a mere scratch ..."

Baqwa, too, is capable of a good body blow to a poor production. "One would have expected the play to at least address the myths and fallacies," he offered, and "teach the youth about choices on the sexual terrain."

In fact, the play succeeded in conveying one message and one message only, Baqwa wrote in his report: "One must use a condom when indulging in sexual activity, otherwise one is bound to contract Aids and die."

Okay, it's a simplistic message but if everyone who watched Sarafina 2 came away with this unequivocal instruction, it was money well spent. Well, perhaps not the full R14,2-million.

Baqwa's idea that this indeed was the message "was borne out by what certain witnesses had to say on their impressions in this regard" during the hearings on the topic.

A representative from an Aids consortium told Baqwa that, in his opinion, the play gave a negative message, and education messages were either weak or seriously deficient.

A "major effort" would be needed to re-evaluate the play's message, Baqwa said. In this effort, "experts in various disciplines should be involved to ensure that the correct message is conveyed in the best possible way".

That should get them flocking to the aisles. I'd stick with the fireworks and the condoms.

I'm looking forward, in the meantime, to his review of the video.

19 CYRIL RAMAPHOSA: 'WAITING FOR THE BIRTH OF THAT CONSTITUTION'

December 9 1996

(As the clock ticks, South Africa's political parties rush to complete the country's new constitution)

It's day zero minus one. Tomorrow the nation and the world will expect South Africa to celebrate its new constitution.

The choir, which will sing the constitutional assembly's anthem in the morning, is practising outside. The red carpets have been laid and the wooden podiums put in place. The four-storey constitutional mural, covered by a white cloth, has been hung on the side of a building across from Tuynhuys.

There is excitement and expectation in the corridors, halls, offices and canteens of the old assembly building.

There is only one problem. The constitution is not ready yet.

As Cyril Ramaphosa, chairman of the constitutional assembly, later confides, "we were getting into a situation where I didn't think we were going to reach an agreement".

President Nelson Mandela tells partygoers at a government function on Wednesday night that he had several speeches prepared for the occasion. "A number of possible alternatives faced our country," he says. "I just hope I've got the right speech".

As has been the case so often in South Africa's constitutional process, waiting becomes the key activity as senior negotiators lock horns behind closed doors.

"Solutions are in the air," Leon Wessels, the assembly deputy chairman, tells a packed chamber just before 5pm. The three remaining issues, the lockout, single-medium education and property clauses, are still undecided.

At 7.10pm, Ramaphosa and Roelf Meyer, the NP's chief negotiator, hold impromptu press conferences on the marble-floored lobby outside the old chamber.

An agreement is imminent, they say: come back at 7.30pm.

At 8.25pm, the assembly is packed once more with MPs, senators, press, lobbyists, and assorted observers.

Ramaphosa, as has become something of a tradition in the latter stages of the constitutional process, starts reading out a joke version of the agreement. "The state will provide no compensation for the expropriation of private property unless it has the willingness and ability," he says, chuckling. Once more, the constitutional committee adjourns.

At 9.30pm and on a more serious note, Ramaphosa announces that an entirely new issue has been brought up - the question of pensions.

The NP, it turns out, has realised only now that pensions for office bearers in the previous government - and struggle pensions[4], as a sweetener - have been left out.

"We are about to finalise this agreement, but there is another consultation that is necessary to seal this. We've been waiting two years, so what's another 20

[4] 'Struggle pensions' refers to the provision in South Africa's constitution for the distribution of payments to "persons or their dependents who made sacrifices or who have served the public interest in the establishment of a democratic constitutional order".

minutes?" he asks.

It is 10.55pm and the old assembly chamber is fuller than it has been all day. In a sense the venue is remarkably appropriate. It was here, among the dark wood benches, green leather seats and thick pile carpets, that the famous "wind of change" speech was delivered, here that the so-called architect of apartheid, Hendrik Verwoerd, was killed. It was also here, 10 years ago that Louis le Grange, then minister of law and order, introduced a motion to proclaim a state of emergency.

The viciousness of what happened after that decision, together with the concerted effort to begin serious negotiations, launched about the same time by Mandela from Robben Island and by the ANC's leadership in exile, was to mark the beginning of the final lap of South Africa's transition to democracy.

Mandela told the Cape Town Press Club on Thursday morning that he had sent a letter to PW Botha, then state president, in July 1986 appealing for talks to begin in earnest.

The main issue at the time was the government's fear that majority rule would result in the domination and subjugation of the white minority.

"How far have we moved since then," he commented wryly.

In the meantime, agreement has been reached. A few hours later, deep now into the morning of day zero, and the last amendments have been clarified. The constitution is ready, just a few hours before the public starts queuing for places in the gallery of the national assembly for the festivities.

Day zero arrives. A yellowing band of smog has gathered over Cape Town. In the distance, the dark silhouette of the mountains looks as if a jagged strip has been torn off the bottom of the horizon.

A helicopter buzzes overhead.

The ubiquitous smiles belie the fatigue and stress of the preceding weeks. General Constand Viljoen, the Freedom Front leader, stares vacantly into the middle distance. Govan Mbeki, the senate deputy speaker, has a beatific smile stamped permanently on his face. He later walks across the chamber with Kobie Coetsee, the senate speaker and one of the first senior NP members to engage in negotiations with the ANC, their arms draped around each other.

Deputy President Thabo Mbeki is as austere and sombre as usual. Nothing betrays the fact that he began writing his speech at 1am. It is a famous speech, Walt Whitmanesque in its phrasing ("the crack and rumble of summer thunders") with the passion and conceptual elegance of Franz Fanon ("It is a unique creation of African hands and African minds, drawing on the accumulated wisdom of all humankind").

The vote itself takes two tries - the electronic voting system is playing up, as usual. But eventually, on time and by an 85 percent majority, South Africa adopts a new constitution.

20 A NEW CONSTITUTION, YET WITH ROOM FOR CHANGE

December 16, 1996

The adoption of the 1996 Constitution of the Republic of South Africa Bill ushers in a new era in South African politics.

But while the basic ground rules of political and societal interaction have been cast in bronze, there remains much room for manoeuvre and change.

A number of "technical" amendments are already being framed to be put to the national assembly and, where they affect the provinces, the senate, in the coming weeks.

As with all amendments, a two-thirds majority is required.

In the words of Nelson Mandela during his celebratory speech following the adoption of the new constitution: "The adoption is only the beginning of our efforts to resolve the problems of this country ... we will continue searching for solutions."

He confirmed later that meetings with various Afrikaner communities had already been scheduled for the coming week.

"There are still concerns on the part of some minorities. We will continue to engage the Freedom Front on those issues they are not happy with."

In his own speech, Freedom Front leader Constand Viljoen told the last meeting of the constitutional assembly that while there were aspects of the document with which his party were not happy, such as the soft clause on single-medium education, it found it impossible to vote against the adoption of the country's new basic law.

With the exception of the African Christian Democratic Party, this was a sentiment echoed by all parties.

Tony Leon, the DP leader, said he was "deeply disappointed" with some areas, and Deputy President FW de Klerk said there was much with which the NP was "not satisfied", and that the party was "even in total disagreement with a number of clauses".

As Willie Hofmeyr, an ANC MP, pointed out during the final hours before adoption: "We do not expect anybody to be very happy with this formula ... but perhaps they will be a little happier knowing how unhappy everybody else is."

Admitting there were "many clauses we didn't like", Mandela said the result was further evidence of the ANC's commitment to rule by consensus.

The party is now in a position, however, to gradually reverse some of the losses it sustained during the negotiation process.

But the institution to have first crack at making changes is the Constitutional Court, which must certify the document before it is officially signed into law.

Some argue that the court will order a number of minor amendments - if only to assert its independence. While it is unlikely to do so on those grounds, there is nothing to stop it forcing wholesale changes to some highly controversial clauses.

The net effect of these dynamics is that, as Cyril Ramaphosa has pointed out many times, the constitution is a "living" document that will evolve over time.

It is not too late for a form of volkstaat, for abortion to be declared illegal, or for lockouts to be reinstated - it is just going to be more difficult to muster the required consensus in the current political environment.

With the NP freed from the culpability of decision-making, we can expect fierce criticism from the opposition benches. While the promise is that this criticism will be "constructive", some royal bun fights are pending in the national assembly.

Just how well the ANC will react to sustained and hostile questioning remains to be seen.

Until now, Mandela and Mbeki were allowed to remain aloof from really nasty jibes. It will soon be open season on both - not to mention the entire cabinet.

And if the rumours are correct that a rightwing backlash within the NP forced the party's withdrawal from the government, the days ahead will be even more highly charged.

It remains to be seen, too, how the Inkatha Freedom Party will react to the events of the week. Perhaps the fact that in effect South Africa has an ANC-IFP coalition in power at the national level will serve to help ease tensions in KwaZulu-Natal.

But interparty dynamics, while governed in broad terms by the constitution, take place at a different level. It will be easier for a party to secure legislative changes with a simple majority than to opt for constitutional amendments.

The constitution is vague enough not to preclude certain legislative developments that would have the same net effect as a constitutional amendment.

Many significant changes characterised the shift from the interim to the final constitution that occurred over the last two years.

From the first words of the pre-amble - which in the interim constitution were "In humble submission to almighty God" and in the final version are "We, the people of South Africa" - the changes are evident.

The main areas include the excising of many transitional arrangements in the original document, such as the creation of the constitutional assembly; the replacement of the Senate by the National Council of Provinces; the refashioning of the clauses on the right to property, labour relations and the environment in the Bill of Rights; and the creation of a commission for the promotion and protection of the rights of cultural, religious and linguistic communities.

Perhaps most critical of all is the scrapping of multiparty government and the entrenchment of simple majority rule.

The NP and the IFP have argued this was how executive decisions were already being taken. But it was mainly because of this issue that the NP decided to leave the coalition.

The constitution ensures that it will not be enough for government simply to refrain from violating people's rights, according to Ramaphosa.

Instead, it provides a framework for sound and effective governance and lays a basis for the continuing transformation of society.

How exactly this will occur is now up to us.

21 PIK BOTHA STANDS DOWN

May 19 1996

(Pik Botha was foreign minister for 26 years and he spent many of those years tilting at political windmills. Twice he stood for prime minister and twice he was defeated. As he steps down, the memories come in a rush.)

Suddenly it is all over, says Pik Botha, leaning forward in his chair with his hands on his thighs.

He is still a big man with a famously gravelly voice and a Brandoesque aura, but there is a sadness now in his body language. He looks tired. He closes his eyes as he drags on his cigarette and the ash simply falls to the carpet.

Through the windows of his 17th floor Plein Street office, the sun is setting over Cape Town.

"I tried to run a video of my life, but I find it difficult to do in a comprehensive way," he says.

He remembers much: the famous altercations, the disasters, the friends, the victories, the defeats. But there is so much to recall, and the video seems to get fuzzy at points, muddle the order or skip over parts.

His defeat this week in trying to persuade the National Party leader, FW de Klerk, not to withdraw from the government was just one more in a line of quixotic bouts he has waged against the windmills of domestic and international opinion.

"It's a very painful experience going into battle knowing you can't win," he says of an all-too-common phenomenon in his long career.

Twice he stood for prime minister and twice he was defeated. He fought economic sanctions but saw them imposed.

Even the post of foreign minister, which he held for 26 years, seemed to bring him into inevitable conflict and opposition with his own superiors and national policy.

"To be a good foreign minister you must be at loggerheads with your government every single day. You have to be, because you are seeing it from outside, from a global perspective".

The comment is a gentle gibe at the current foreign minister, Alfred Nzo, and the lack of neutrality Botha believes characterises South Africa's foreign policy.

"We should have decided on a policy of neutrality - it's still not too late. We should tell our ambassador to the United Nations to abstain in any dispute. This is a viable alternative, and I would have thought the world would have understood."

But his words also confirm the rumours that he never really saw eye to eye with De Klerk.

"We're from different schools of thought. He was more conservative than I was," he says.

The National Party itself would have to change radically, including its name, to rid itself finally of his history and muster a more substantial level of black support, he says.

"The NP still carries the burden, the luggage - I see it and feel it every day."

A more general political regrouping in which the "unnatural alliance" of the ANC, the South African Communist Party and Cosatu would be broken up and the racially based Freedom Front dismantled is "inevitable as we move away from the bitterness of the past".

But along with the disappointments of the past are stacked the achievements. And it is on these in particular he will dwell when he retires from the public service.

They include the signing of the Nkomati Accord in 1984, the withdrawal of Cuban troops from Angola and the subsequent independence of Namibia, his seven appearances before the UN Security Council, his "painful but crucial" role in Zimbabwe's independence, his friendships with Margaret Thatcher, Lord Carrington, Ronald Reagan, Henry Kissinger and other world leaders, and the signing of the nuclear non-proliferation treaty.

You get the impression he could talk endlessly about the adventures and tales of his life in the world of international diplomacy and politics.

He tells of the time he was smuggled through the back door of the White House to meet Reagan; of the moment when he so infuriated the Soviet representative on the UN Security Council that the representative smashed his fist on the table, breaking the intercom system; of Kissinger carving his initials into a marula tree.

But now it is time to pack up his things and think about the future. Along with his party's decision to leave government - which will involve him finding a new house and car appropriate for a back bencher - his wife's death only two weeks ago was a further blow for him to come to terms with.

In the immediate future, Botha has two offices, a house and his ministerial portfolio of mineral and energy affairs to vacate.

Then he will spend time unpacking his books in his Pretoria house, "get down to sorting things out" and begin writing a book.

In the meantime, he will make himself available for consultancy or mediation work, either here or internationally.

Beyond his office windows, it is almost dark now. With his departure, South Africa's political firmament is a little duller tonight.

22 EUGENE DE KOCK[5] OPENS A PANDORA'S BOX

September 22 1996

Like a drunken cowboy staggering down a dusty street, mortally wounded but firing wildly and blindly in all directions, Eugene de Kock has caused panic and consternation in the last days of his infamous trial.

As random bullets have broken bordello windows and brought down chandeliers in the saloon, so too they have winged prominent townsfolk in volley after volley of allegation, rumour and gossip.

While tragic and macabre at the best of times, the De Kock trial this week has been scintillating theatre prodding all sorts of famous people into seeking legal advice or scrambling to host urgent press conferences.

Among the luminaries to take direct hits have been FW De Klerk, PW Botha, Bantu Holomisa (who seemingly is never far from a good story these days), Tokyo Sexwale, Winnie Mandela, Chris Ball, Themba Khoza, Adriaan Vlok and Pik Botha.

Not bad work for a week in the witness box. And that excludes half the police force, current and retired, who have also been named during the course of this

[5] Eugene De Kock was to confess to hundreds of murders at the Truth and Reconciliation Commission. Nicknamed "Prime Evil" for his leadership of state death-squads, he was sentenced to 212 years and two life terms in 1996. He served 20 years before being paroled.

week's court proceedings.

Now that he has pleaded guilty to 89 serious crimes, including several murder charges, it seems De Kock has nothing left to lose.

Few, even of his latest list of victims, will be able to deny all the allegations.

This is where De Kock is so dangerous. It is difficult to tell how much is fact and how much fabrication.

Holomisa, for instance, agrees with De Kock that the Pretoria regime was intent on destabilising his little kingdom in the Eastern Cape. But, of course, he stops short of conceding he had anything to do with the execution of the leader of an attempted coup.

De Klerk agrees with De Kock that he personally authorised a 1993 SADF raid in Transkei but stops short of confirming his own cowardice and greed.

Perhaps the juiciest gossip of all concerned allegations about Winnie Mandela's so-called sex slave.

De Kock alleged Johannes Magota, Mandela's driver and bodyguard, had also performed various other duties - under duress. Reference to these duties, as well as to his attributes, had been captured on tape.

"I at first did not believe him, but Captain Anton Pretorius, who listened to the tapes, said he (Magota) was a man of Olympic standards who would satisfy any woman," the former head of Vlakplaas, told the Pretoria Supreme Court.

Winnie, understandably, is outraged and reported to be seeking legal advice. But I suspect that the prospect of a court action will deter from proceeding into litigation.

In any case, what difference will a libel conviction make to a man who has already confessed to an astonishing list of murders and mayhem?

Frankly, I doubt he cares. One can't help but assume, given De Kock's loquacity on the stand, that some deal has been struck that will ensure he serves no serious time for his crimes.

Still, whether fact or fiction, De Kock's evidence has truly thrown open a Pandora's box of South African dirty tricks.

Like a spider at the centre of his web, De Kock has strings of intrigue reaching into the most secret, most villainous corners of apartheid's dark past.

Perhaps it is best for everyone if all this stuff is brought out now, to be proved or disproved. It forms part of the rich tapestry of our heritage and in its expression will assist in the reconciliation and national unity we all so desperately desire.

Now, where did I put that darn six-shooter?

23 MANDELA: 'THAT'S WHAT MY BOSSES HAVE GIVEN ME TO READ'

December 13 1996

There was a time, when he was still relatively new to the presidency, that Nelson Mandela seldom deviated from the carefully prepared speeches handed to him by his staff.

It was only when he removed his spectacles - usually half-way through an address - paused for a moment and looked out at his audience, that you knew he was about to break off from the text and speak his mind.

A casual glance at the presidential aides, sinking deeper and deeper into their chairs as the president warmed to his new topic, was ample confirmation that a Mandelaism was afoot.

More often than not, it was former president FW De Klerk who bore the brunt of these remarks.

These days, Mandela has adopted a slightly different approach. Now he reads through the text and upon completion, says something like: "Well, that's what my bosses have given me to read. Now I will speak about what I really feel".

The latest example of one of his postscripts came during the signing of the Constitution in Sharpeville earlier this week.

After his formal, at times almost lyrical address ("Out of the many Sharpevilles which haunt our history..."), Mandela once again wandered off into story-telling mode.

Picking out Defence Minister Joe Modise in the crowd, Mandela talked of the time he and "JM" broke up a Communist Party meeting in the mid-1940s.

Modise was Mandela's bodyguard and briefcase carrier in the early days of the armed struggle.

He was also the one, on that particular night, who pushed Mandela on to the stage to get on with his task of sabotaging the meeting.

He achieved this by resorting to emotionalism - an example, he said, of how easy it was to distract people from logic and truth by appealing to their passions and fears.

As usual, Mandela's tales have a moral and a message.

However, like all world leaders and a high proportion of senior local politicians, Mandela rarely writes his own speeches.

The really big-event addresses are generally prepared by his deputy, Thabo Mbeki.

Mbeki, whose "I am an African" speech was undoubtedly one of the orations of the year, was responsible for Mandela's speeches to the United Nations General Assembly at the time of South Africa's readmittance, the Houses of Parliament at Westminster earlier this year; the US Congress in 1994, the opening of Parliament "state of the nation" speeches in February each year and a number of othe key addresses.

Mandela, of course, sees drafts of all his speeches and inevitably has corrections and amendments to add, according to his staff.

This, combined with his propensity to ad lib, gives his addresses the personal touch.

For the main part, though, the process is that the department, ministry or organisation concerned prepares a rough draft, the presidential staff - mainly the highly regarded former editor of Mayibuye and now key presidential aide Joel Netshitenzhe - draws up a second draft and a final version is put together with input from Mbeki and from the president himself. These are the "bosses" to whom Mandela refers when he has finished delivering his text.

However, Mandela is a man who simply loves to talk, tell stories and reminisce. Even away from the glare of the cameras and far from the demands of high office, he is irrepressible in his enthusiasm to chat and tell tales.

So, while it is probably comforting to know that our next president is an extremely gifted speech writer, there are still another two years of opportunities for Mandela to lay his text aside and go off for a while on his own path.

24 IS A RIGHTWING COUP STILL POSSIBLE?

January 8, 1997

For years now, the threat of a violent rightwing uprising has formed an intimate part of the backdrop of South African political life.

It was the threat of such an occurrence that aided the National Party in its "Yes" referendum victory back in 1992 - you may remember the ubiquitous posters of ominous-looking balaclava-clad Ystergaarders above the caption: "Don't leave your future in this man's hands." It helped secure the "Yes" victory in the last whites-only poll.

In late 1995, a book entitled *The Mini-Nuke Conspiracy* by Peter Hounan and Steve McQuillan, claimed the rightwing not only had a squadron of impala jets and a battery of C5 cannons in its possession, but had access to nuclear weaponry too.

These fears, with various thefts from state arsenals and a number of high-profile right-wing actions, including the storming of the World Trade Centre by the Afrikaner Weerstandsbeweging, served to keep the right-wing *gevaar* (threat) high on the national political agenda.

But the writing was really on the wall for the right-wing from the moment its charismatic leader, Eugene TerreBlanche, fell off his horse.

The discrediting of TerreBlanche (by his own tabloid exploits); the death, at around the same time, of Conservative Party stalwart Andries Treurnicht; and the emergence of a new, moderate Afrikaner political voice - that of General Constand Viljoen - seemed to take the wind out of the extreme rightwing's sails.

The final straw, in March 1994, appeared to be the disastrous intervention of the Right's forces in Bophuthatswana during the coup which overthrew Lucas Mangope.

The affair, in which three AWB members were gunned down by Bop troops in full view of the world media, suggested that the extreme right was a force of fat couch potatoes with a grudge rather than any real threat to national security or democracy.

In the few weeks before the April 1994 election, however, the ultra-right quickly showed how seriously it needed to be taken.

At least 20 people died, and dozens were injured in the pre-election bombing spree that swept across Gauteng.

"Our biggest problem," Freedom Front chief secretary Flip Buys told the press this week, "is that Afrikaners have no culture of lawful protest".

Among the many arrests at the time were three former Ystergaard members, Nicolaas Barnard, Abraham Myburgh and Jan de Wet.

After being convicted, the three were awaiting sentence when they contrived to escape from Diepkloof prison in March last year.

Since their escape, President Nelson Mandela has agreed to the extension of the amnesty period from December 1993 to May 1994. This meant all three were eligible for full amnesty and would likely have been released.

Instead, they opted for a life on the run. Now up for escaping, they are among the chief suspects for the Christmas bombings in Worcester.

The evidence, from the splintered and ineffectual state of the extreme Right over the last couple of years, does not really suggest a co-ordinated campaign.

Rather, it indicates a few extremists, perhaps disgruntled and bitter, looking for an outlet for their frustrations.

In intelligence circles, they are being referred to as "weekender" radicals.

"Weekenders are people who strongly believe in a rightwing cause but are not part of a military or terrorist organisation," an intelligence spokesman explained last week.

"They are known as weekenders because they gather in small groups to discuss their beliefs over drinks and one sentiment leads to another, which is enough to stir action."

The truth behind the Worcester and Rustenburg bombings has yet to be uncovered, though several suspects have already been arrested for both sets of attacks.

Is some larger conspiracy likely to be unveiled? From the evidence so far, this is improbable.

While it is difficult to underplay events which cost human lives, it is just as easy to exaggerate the actions of a few madmen.

It takes only one lunatic with a pipe full of ammonia nitrate to send a chill down the national spine. But this doesn't necessarily mean a rightwing coup is imminent.

25 BY-ELECTION DAY IN BOKSBURG

October 19 1997

It is another quiet weekday afternoon at the Black Marlin Action Bar in Boksburg. Under the crumbling portals of the old Central Hotel, in which the Black Marlin shelters its anonymous, solidary clients, a few prostitutes chat idly on the pavement.

Sheltered from a gloomy highveld sky, they scan the infrequent Commissioner Street traffic with an air of crushing boredom.

Across the road, beyond the pink blush of the newly painted city hall, the agents of another of the world's oldest profession, politics, go about their business with equal lethargy.

It is municipal by-election day in Boksburg and mid-afternoon fewer than 50 voters have bothered to turn up.

In the caravans and tents of the six parties contesting the seat, unopened trays of sandwiches sweat under clingwrap.

"It's all very quiet but I'm sure the people will come after work," says one plump young woman in the Conservative Party tent who sits in the heat with her head in her hands. In the background, boeremusik softens the beat of the more modern sounds emanating from the ANC booth.

While the CP only managed to secure 125 votes this time round, the party was once the ruling power in this East Rand town. After defeating the incumbent National Party in the 1988 local government poll, the new CP council gained Boksburg instant notoriety.

Within days the council announced it would be applying the rules and regulations of petty apartheid, particularly the Separate Amenities Act, with determination and vigour. What followed was almost six years of racial conflict, boycotts, demonstrations, and violent clashes that embarrassed the government and highlighted the ironies and absurdities of own-area ideology.

The locus of much of this bitter strife was the Boksburg Lake, a five-minute stroll from the Black Marlin.

In 1888, Montagu White arrived in Boksburg to take up his post as the new administrative officer in charge of the Boksburg goldfields.

To say the least he was disappointed by the state of the town at that stage. He wrote that Boksburg "struck me as being one of the most uninviting spots I have ever seen".

From his window at the hotel - and the odds are pretty good it was the Central - "not a tree or shrub was to be seen".

In fact, history suggests there was only one tree then in the 15-mile area that is now central Boksburg. This was referred to as "the Boksburg Forest".

The presence of the Cason mine dump would also give the town the tag of being, literally, the biggest dump in the southern hemisphere.

It was Montagu who gained permission from President Paul Kruger to establish the man-made lake around which so much more of the town's history was to be contested.

One of the first actions taken by the colourful CP council - some of whose members were later accused of a whole range of offences from planting bombs at the Rand Show and electoral fraud to the planned assassination of FW De

Klerk, Nelson Mandela, and the local NP MP, Sakkie Blanché - was the erection of an expensive fence around the lake.

Though De Klerk was soon to scrap the Separate Amenities Act, the council's application of the act to the town's library, swimming pool and other facilities made it universally synonymous with racism and apartheid.

Incensed by the council's stance, the community at Reiger Park launched a year-long boycott of white business in Boksburg which brought the town, and eventually its council, to its knees.

The defiance campaign also targeted the lake where protest picnics invoked the wrath of the rightwing, particularly the Afrikaner Weerstandsbeweging. Bloody clashes, police actions and violence followed.

But even in the midst of the conflict the signs of change were evident. The defiance campaign was a significant factor in De Klerk's decision to scrap the Separate Amenities Act.

Windmill Park, on the outskirts of the town - which was proclaimed a city in 1992 - was the site of one of the first legal 'grey areas' in South Africa. In 1989, De Klerk declared the CBD a free trading area. The move was described by one CP councillor as "the beginning of the end for white South Africa."

Back at the Black Marlin, a single battered old Ford pulls up and collects one of the women before speeding off down Commissioner Street. Business is beginning to pick up.

26 FW DE KLERK: SAYING GOODBYE TO POLITICS

November 9 1997

It's a warm Saturday afternoon in Pretoria's Laudium suburb and Tangerine Street is buzzing with life.

Just down from the sparkling white mosque and across from Mohideen's takeaway and the Sitaar bottle store, a familiar figure is stooped over, lighting a cigarette. As he pauses a moment to breathe in deeply and look around, people wander over to shake his hand and chat for a moment or two.

FW De Klerk, looking elegantly casual in a light grey suit, is in Laudium to bid farewell to the National Party faithful after more than three decades of service.

"This is where I cut my political teeth," he later tells the 500 delegates to the NP's fourth annual provincial congress in Gauteng.

But Vereeniging, where De Klerk practiced as an attorney and was first elected as a member of parliament in 1972, is a far cry from Laudium.

It is unlikely, for instance, that in all his years of speechifying at NP provincial congresses, De Klerk has ever been interrupted by midday prayers from a neighbouring mosque.

And while the party's famous koeksisters were in evidence at the post-congress do, I doubt any former NP assemblies were kicked off by Indian dancers doing a version of the macarena.

But politics moves on and parties battle to reinvent and reinvigorate themselves in the eternal bid for popular support. Certainly, the NP has suffered some fearful blows in the last few months. De Klerk's own departure ("I know my resignation was a shock," he admits later), the decampment of the party's Sir Launcelot, Roelf Meyer, a succession of heavy by-election defeats and the defection of a number of senior party officials have left the organisation floundering.

It remains to be seen whether it will survive with the young, ambitious Marthinus van Schalkwyk at the helm and only 18 months to the next election.

By sheer coincidence, a sign hangs on a doorway in the grounds of the Laudium Community Centre saying "Emergency and Disaster Management".

This is no reference to current party strategy, and yet there is more than just a hint of crisis at the proceedings within.

"I have attended NP congresses from my school years when I went with my father as a delegate for the first time in 1962, until now, and in all those years the party specifically in this part of the country, had to manage considerable challenges," De Klerk says in his address.

"There were tremendous setbacks, like the split in 1982 when this congress elected me as leader after Treurnicht and his band left the NP. We are going through some of this again, though it is not as serious and not about the same issues."

While De Klerk obviously takes an interest in these developments and promises to act as a grandfather to the party, his time is now over.

"Didn't I always look relaxed?" he asks me, a light breeze rustling the palm trees on Tangerine Street.

"Actually, no."

In fact, while he looks as comfortable as one can appear in a suit under the hot highveld sun, De Klerk, now 61, has aged considerably in the past few months. His skin, while never particularly smooth, is flakier now and his nose deeply veined.

Perhaps for some the cut and thrust of national politics is an elixir for vigour and youthful hard work, the adrenalin a drug-like necessity for the long hours of heated debate. But when one has dismounted the mustang of destiny, the paddock can be a quiet place.

De Klerk is writing a book now about his experiences and is travelling the world giving speeches. He recently returned from a four-lecture tour of the United States and will shortly be embarking on a further run on the global circuit.

"To a certain extent this is an emotional moment for all of us," said new Gauteng NP leader Sam de Beer, somewhat ambiguously, of De Klerk's imminent arrival on stage in Laudium. But when it came to the presentation of the gift, the official responsible was nowhere to be seen.

"Has anybody seen Mr Watusi?" De Beer asked plaintively. Before long, the aforesaid Mr Watusi arrived. "I was called by nature," he apologised before handing a long, steel bar with wrapping paper wound round the top to the former leader of the National Party and the country.

De Klerk, perhaps thinking for a moment of what needed to be done to some of the party organisers in the wake of the by-election defeats, was quick to point out: "It's not a knobkerrie, it's a golf club."

27 FAREWELL TAIWAN, HELLO BEIJING!

December 14 1997

On a sulty summer night this week in Waterkloof, Pretoria, South Africa's bold and beautiful assembled in their cocktail dresses and lounge suits to bid farewell to an old friend.

The old friend was the last ambassador to this country for the Republic of Taiwan, I-cheng Loh.

Unceremoniously dumped by President Nelson Mandela in November last year, when Taipei was cast aside and Bejing embraced, the debonair ambassador was humble and gracious in his adieu.

Before him, arrayed in the humid heat beneath the twirling fans of the Pretoria Country Club's ballroom, a collection of familiar characters clutched wine glasses and spring rolls and paid tribute to the end of an era.

Former foreign minister Pik Botha hugged Winnie Madikizela-Mandela; home affairs minister Mangosuthu Buthelezi held court with a phalanx of his MPs; Freedom Front leader Constand Viljoen and United Democratic Movement co-leader Roelf Meyer rubbed shoulders; while defence minister Joe Modise was seen scuttling from the function before the official speeches had begun.

The turnout, which included a clutch of admirals, MPs, generals, press and ambassadors, was ample evidence of the impact the Taiwanese have had in South Africa during the years in which they enjoyed full diplomatic recognition.

Many theories abound as to why Mandela made that shock announcement in the garden of his home in Houghton, Johannesburg, in January.

Certainly, few were expecting it, least of all the Taiwanese.

Some say that the imminent handover of Hong Kong to the People's Republic of China, and with it hugely important South African economic interests, was a key factor in the switch.

Others argue that potential arms and strategic deals with the largest and second most powerful nation in the world were offered as an incentive.

One of the most convincing theories, however, has to do with the election this year of Kofi Annan as secretary general of the United Nations.

The theory suggests pressure was placed on the African lobby at the UN: if South Africa failed to switch its allegiance from Taiwan then a Chinese veto would deny Africa its first black UN secretary general. African leaders then turned the screws on us and, two weeks before Annan's election, Mandela caved in.

Mandela himself is tight-lipped on the whole affair, saying only that he was "not obliged" to divulge the real reasons.

Two nights after the gathering of the VIPs at the country club, and little more than a 10-minute walk away, the beneficiaries of Mandela's switch held their own cocktail party.

In a palatial, white-walled Waterkloof Ridge mansion, surrounded by verdant palms and dripping shrubbery, the newly appointed ambassador-to-be of the People's Republic of China, Wang Xue Xian, held his own reception.

But where dignitaries wandered the lush gardens of the country club on a still, hot Tuesday night, on Thursday night a highveld storm that would have kept King Lear indoors raged about us - lightning crackled, thunder boomed, and torrential rain pounded the patio.

But what the evening lacked in clear skies and VIPs - it was admittedly, only a press night - it made up for in the superlative food and Great Wall wine that had been laid on for 60 guests (only 20 pitched).

Wang, fresh from his post as deputy head of China's mission at the UN in New York, was also debonair and gracious. Obviously very senior, he seemed a little bemused at his posting from the coalface of international relations to the somewhat less substantial southern tip of Africa.

Still, the jacarandas were out when he arrived, the sun was shining and the Taiwanese had been sent packing from another global outpost, even if Loh did leave with an Order of Good Hope in his pocket.

Wang's bemusement has no doubt been tempered, though, by the imminent arrival of a very high-ranking delegation from Beijing and, of course, by the consolation of a full ambassadorship.

28 KADER ASMAL: BRINGING BACK DEATH PENALTY LIKE 'RIDING A TIGER'

August 30 1998

There would probably be a fair amount of support in South Africa for the suggestion I heard in the corridors of Parliament this week that the perpetrators of the Planet Hollywood bombing should be marched off to Greenmarket Square and beheaded in public.

But not far from where these furtive whisperings of revenge and retribution were taking place, Parliament was debating the issue of capital punishment in more sober terms.

The National Party, which led South Africa in its time to the lofty height of the world's most enthusiastic judicial executioner, says that more than 70 percent of ordinary South Africans are in favour of the death penalty.

Even Kader Asmal, the minister of water affairs, conceded that "almost everywhere in the world there is, among the populace at large, a strong feeling in favour of the judicial killing of certain offenders".

Why, then, in the face of such overwhelming public support, does the government choose to ignore the will of its citizens, particularly when that government claims to lead a newly democratic state?

"The ANC is afraid of public opinion," claimed Sheila Camerer, the former NP deputy justice minister, who admitted that she had undergone something of a Damascene conversion on the question of capital punishment since she opposed it in 1993.

The debate on whether to hold a referendum was called for by the Inkatha Freedom Party, which has also done a policy about-face on the issue.

In 1995, the IFP voted against the NP proposal that just such a referendum be held. This week it proposed the very same thing.

Unsurprisingly, ANC speakers - including Dullah Omar, the minister of justice - accused the IFP of rank electioneering in the wake of the public outrage against the Planet Hollywood atrocity.

But while the question at hand, on the surface at least, was the desirability of otherwise of restoring the death penalty - which, it will be recalled, the Constitutional Court has already deemed to be unconstitutional on the grounds that it is "cruel and inhumane" - the real issue is whether or not a referendum is a desirable method of changing the constitution.

Surely if a substantial majority of citizens say unequivocally in a referendum that they want the constitution changed, that desire should be acknowledged by the political representatives of that majority?

Instead of the death penalty, though, let us say that a referendum is proposed calling for all privately owned property to be returned to the state for redistribution, in equal portions, to all the citizens of South Africa.

Unquestionably, the overwhelming majority of South Africans would heartily endorse it. So, should the constitution's property rights clause be changed?

What about a referendum on whether Die Stem should be retained in the national anthem, or whether Afrikaans or Zulu should continue to be official languages?

Again, there is little doubt what the majority would choose. Does that make it right to rewrite the constitution to reflect the wishes of the majority?

Asmal, who lectured on constitutional law for many years at Trinity College, Dublin, argued that a referendum would set an "awful precedent".

Such a referendum, in the wake of Planet Hollywood, "would be riding on the back of real anger and fear among the public. It would be riding on the back of a tiger". In fact, an important part of the constitution's role in our new society was to protect minorities from the tyranny of the majority, it was even "anti-majoritarian", claimed Asmal.

"True democracy does not necessarily allow the majority to rule on all subjects". But even as a referendum was effectively quashed in Parliament this week, the clamour for the death penalty grows ever louder.

Fuelled by events at Cape Town's Waterfront, opposition politicians - now joined by the IFP - added their kindling to the fire. "Talk will not take us anywhere," railed Marthinus van Schalkwyk, leader of the National Party.

"Criminals feel they can do anything in our country and get away with it. The ANC argues that murderers have human rights, but about the victims?"

The IFP, warming to its new message, argued that while it had resolutely opposed violence as a means of solving political problems, "life has become so cheap in the South Africa of today", said Eldred Ferreira, one of its MPs.

That is an important point, even if it wasn't the one intended by Ferreira. Life has not only become cheap recently in South Africa, it has been cheap for decades. Apartheid made sure of that.

It is the cheapness of, and disrespect for, life that fuels domestic violence, that leads to the killing of police officers for their guns, that causes drivers to be executed for their vehicles, that encourages those drivers to speed and drink on the highways and that underpins the insane pipe-bomb attacks that have terrorised Capetonians in recent months.

The South African state should be doing all it can to value and celebrate human life, not give official sanction to mob vengeance by ending life with the alacrity and brutality so characteristic of the criminals that it seeks to overcome.

29 VAN SCHALKWYK: DESPERATE TO STOP THE NP SINKING

September 13 1998

A year ago, Marthinus van Schalkwyk took over from FW de Klerk as leader of the National Party.

Filling the shoes of "Papa" de Klerk, as his faithful supporters called him, was likely to be no easy task, particularly when signs of the party's deteriorating fortunes were even then becoming evident.

De Klerk had already baulked at undertaking the kind of reforms within the party that would give it life in the new dispensation. He had pulled the party out of the cabinet, affording his successor little opportunity to make any impact other than as a leader of the opposition. He had declined to scrap the NP name and begin afresh without the overwhelming baggage of apartheid. He had chased off his key reformer, Roelf Meyer and pandered to the old timers.

Rather like WIlliam Hague following John Major as the leader of the Conservative Party in Britain, the Titanic had a new hand on the helm - but it was still the Titanic.

Van Schalkwyk has done what he can to right the ship. He has urged greater co-operation between opposition parties, he has reshuffled and diversified the party leadership and he has toured the country speaking to potential voters.

But all this has been to little avail.

His plans for an opposition alliance at the next election have crumbled, a rash of defections and resignations has crippled his party structures, the unstinting support of church and Afrikaner cultural organisations has been lost, important municipal by-elections have ended in resounding defeats and the party's popularity at the polls has slipped alarmingly from 24 percent in 1994 to less than 10 percent.

To many observers, the party is doomed. Next year it will be lucky to retain its status as the official opposition. At the general election in 2004, the NP may not exist at all.

But in the face of such dire predictions, Van Schalkwyk remains upbeat about the party's future, as well as his own. "When I entered politics in 1990, I was prepared for this. I knew that being in opposition was going to be hard," he said this week.

There are few, admittedly very few, factors that suggest the NP will not be totally crushed in May next year: With up to R30-million to spend on the election campaign, a number of disillusioned or undecided voters and no serious contender to the ANC in sight, many voters could yet be persuaded to stick with what they know.

But the bad signs just keep on building. The recent defection to Bantu Holomisa's United Democratic Movement of the Gauteng NP leader Sam de Beer, was a damaging blow.

On Thursday, the NP gave up another of its cast-iron wards, this time at Grassy Park in the Cape, to the ANC.

Van Schalkwyk insists, however, that all is not as gloomy as it appears.

In 1994, De Klerk visited the former homeland town of Giyani and was promptly stoned by angry onlookers. Earlier this month, Van Schalkwyk spoke there to a full house. "About 40 percent came to listen and 60 percent were very enthusiastic," he said.

Whether or not anyone else in the party could have done a better job as leader - NP KwaZulu-Natal leader Danie Schutte and De Beer were Van Schalkwyk's main opponents for the job - is a moot point.

The party simply cannot shake off its apartheid roots and the legacy of its devastating policies. It probably doesn't matter who has their hands on the helm. The ship is still going down.

30 TRUTH COMMISSION: TIME WILL VINDICATE IT

October 25 1998

I will never forget that sunny day in East London back in early 1996 when the Truth and Reconciliation Commission held its first public hearing into human rights abuses during the apartheid era.

A fresh sea breeze rippled the commission banner on the front of the quaint city hall; police officers gathered by their vehicles in the street and the wooden floors echoed with the sound of lawyers, journalists, interpreters, victims, commissioners, and the public gathering to launch a new phase in South African history.

The truth commission is something of which we can be immensely proud. Yes, it has been controversial. Yes, there have been claims of bias and inadequacy. Yes, there have been mistakes and omissions.

Many will argue, too, that the whole process, which has gone on for two years and ten months, has damaged rather than improved national reconciliation.

But time will vindicate the architects of the truth commission. Of that I have no doubt whatsoever.

That was apparent from the start, when the first victims stood up before the community to say, "this is what happened to me".

There was no mistaking the burdens being lifted, the past being laid to rest, by the acknowledgement and empathy of Archbishop Desmond Tutu and his team.

Fortunately, much more has been achieved. We have learnt of inconceivable atrocities. We have found charred bodies, and buried heroes with dignity. We have uncovered villains and unveiled the apartheid we all knew was there but dared not contemplate in its full dimensions.

The genesis of the truth commission goes much further back, though than those first few hearings.

In the 1970s, the ANC in exile began compiling dossiers on key apartheid leaders with a view to launching a series of Nuremberg trials on achieving liberation.

But the collapse of several military dictatorships in Latin America spawned a new trend. Truth commissions, in various guises and forms, were established in a dozen countries. Principles, guidelines and case studies were compiled, and experience showed that voluntary confessions were more likely to produce results than expensive legal battles.

The victims, too, were far less likely to achieve the kind of attention due to them faced by lawyers and judges than a panel of representative and compassionate commissioners.

The result, after countless hours of negotiation and refinement, is a process admired the world over.

On Thursday this coming week, the commission will present its final report to President Nelson Mandela.

It will be the culmination of a very tough period of national catharsis, of mudslinging and accusation, of tears and bitter recollection.

And though the commission continues its work, ploughing through the thousands of amnesty applications and providing reparation to victims, its task now is more or less complete. It is for the courts to root out the remaining rotten eggs and cast them into the pits of the penal system.

And perhaps now, with our second democratic election on the horizon, we can move on from the viciousness and despair of those times and look to the new century with hope and curiosity in our hearts.

31 CONSTAND VILJOEN: THE AFRIKANER PEOPLE WANT A HOME

November 8 1998

Plans are afoot to launch an Afrikaner alliance ahead of the election next year in a bid to attract 51 percent of the Afrikaner vote, according to Constand Viljoen, the Freedom Front leader.

In an interview, Viljoen said that securing the vote of more than half the 1.8-million registered Afrikaner voters would enable the alliance to push far more effectively for a *volkstaat*.

"Our progress towards a *volkstaat* has been hampered by the perception that the Freedom Front represents a minority of a minority," Viljoen said.

"An Afrikaner alliance would ensure that with 51 percent of the community's support, we would be speaking from a position of strength and the ANC would not be able to ignore us."

Viljoen said that little progress had been made towards the establishment of a *volkstaat* over the past two years.

"This has damaged us a lot. It hasn't allowed us to deliver. Like the ANC, we've also got a delivery problem."

However, he conceded that perhaps more time was needed between the end of apartheid and the promotion of self-determination, which was still regarded by many as a racist concept. "Self-determination is people and culture oriented. It's not racism or physical. It's deeper. It's about intrinsic values, culture, history," he said.

Viljoen said talks about the formation of an Afrikaner alliance had already begun with a view to "consolidating Afrikaner support into something bigger".

It was envisaged that several parties would co-operate to form an alliance, each retaining its own specific ideas but linked by a common commitment to a volkstaat.

"The Afrikaner people want a home," he said.

The election was expected to see the creation of two or three new parties aimed at capturing the Afrikaner vote.

"There's a group in Potchefstroom who are thinking of establishing a political party at the moment," he said.

But the Freedom Front, meanwhile, has been working hard at setting itself up as the primary voice of the community.

In a draft resolution before Parliament earlier this week, Freedom Front MP Pieter Mulder called on the House to note that his party "is becoming the political home of the Afrikaner".

Viljoen said discussions about the notion of an alliance were still in the early stages.

32 TREVOR MANUEL IS NOBODY'S SUCKER

November 8 1998

There's an old saying among poker players that goes: "If you look round the table and can't see who the sucker is, it's you."

Though politics and poker may appear to have little in common, there are some similarities. Who can doubt, for instance, that bluffing, and deceit, false bravado and blind luck are as much factors of life in the body politic as boring speeches and policy statements.

The mini-debates, or interpellations, held in Parliament each Wednesday afternoon provide a good opportunity for opposition parties to spot the sucker and pick on cabinet ministers suffering embarrassment in their portfolios or not articulate enough to defend themselves.

Interpellations last 15 minutes: plenty of time to make your point, have the relevant minister stuttering and flee with a few chips to show off to your voters. The problem comes when you pick the wrong sucker and the sucker ends up being you.

And so it was this week at the last sitting of the 1998 parliamentary session.

Casting an idle eye round the benches as the interpellations warmed up, I couldn't help but notice the figure of Ngila Muendane, the deputy leader of the PAC. He looked anxious and fidgety, wringing his fingers and glaring ahead with all the focus of a 100-metre sprinter waiting for the gun. A glance at the order paper indicated he was soon to take on none other than Professor Kader Asmal, the water affairs and forestry minister, on corruption.

Now, there are good ministers to take on in a debate and there are bad ministers. Stella Sigcau is a cinch, Penuell Maduna gets all flustered and emotional and Sibusiso Bengu is a treat. But Asmal? It was like Baby Jake lining up Mike Tyson, and the results could only be gruesome.

Muendane got the first crack. Corruption was as rampant in the country as it was in the ANC, he charged. "The example the ANC is setting is actually motivating citizens to take up crime," he argued.

The ANC was creating companies to fund its election campaign "using taxpayers' money", land was being bonded to foreigners, administration in Mpumulanga was a mess.

"We need a framework of morality and morality is one of the five principles we've decided are going to make the PAC a model organisation."

Asmal stood, bemused. Corruption is a matter for the justice minister; but Asmal is not one to shy away from a good opportunity to humble the opposition, even if it is the PAC.

"The honourable member has the extraordinary capacity of carrying incoherence and illiteracy to fine levels," he began, to sniggers from the government's benches.

Muendane's statements were "nonsensical", said Asmal, warming to the task. The Mpumulanga provincial government had suspended its finance minister that day over allegations of corruption, a whole range of new laws had been introduced to crack down on criminal syndicates, stop money-laundering and enforce ethics among the executive.

Not only that, but South Africa was the first country in the world to establish a permanent unit, under Judge Willem Heath, to investigate corruption in government.

"We are not claiming there has been no corruption since 1994. This is a corrupt country, but we must start on the right route," said Asmal.

After 15 minutes of articulate pummelling, there was little doubt who the sucker was.

The same was true when NP leader Marthinus Van Schalkwyk chose to go for finance minister Trevor Manuel.

Now Manuel, too, enjoys a good verbal brawl and none more so than when it is at the expense of the leader of the opposition.

Van Schalkwyk came up with the rather biting technique of going through the ANC's election manifesto for 1994, trashing each objective as he went.

Jobs, crime, protecting the disadvantaged, such as women and youth, housing, education - progress in each had been a terrible deceit, Van Schalkwyk contended.

"That manifesto - ANC: A Better Life for All, has been a misnomer. It should have been: A Better Life for ANC politicians - your guide to international travel," which was quite witty, coming from Van Schalkwyk.

But again, and in spite of recent economic hardships, Manuel is nobody's sucker. And with the backing of the larger and more vocal government benches, he proceeded to turn the tables.

"There are none so blind as will not see, none so deaf as will not hear and none so thick as the National Party," he rounded off, looking very pleased with himself.

So, the final week of the 1998 parliamentary session has come and gone and with it the last chance this year for South Africa's parliamentarians to have a good dig at each other in public and on a shared platform.

Certainly, the cudgels will be taken up once more as the elections loom, but at least there is life at the heart of our new democracy. The question of who the sucker is, though, will only be decided when the cards have been laid, the ballots have been counted and the people have had their say.

33 MAX SISULU: REMEMBERING THE CHAOS OF SA'S FIRST DEMOCRATIC PARLIAMENT

November 1 1998

Max Sisulu smiles ruefully when he remembers the first few months of South Africa's first democratic Parliament in 1994.

None of the new intake of more than 300 ANC parliamentarians had any experience in the institution, they knew little of law-making or of committee work, offices were bare and resources were meagre. "There weren't even computers in the offices. Nobody knew what to do. It was chaos," says Sisulu, the ANC's chief whip.

With the last week of the current parliamentary year starting tomorrow, Sisulu can look back with some pride at developments over the past four years and begin preparations for the next group of MPs due to make the trip south in the Autumn.

So much has changed since May 1994. The old portraits, statues and symbols of apartheid have been replaced with colourful, often abstract, paintings and artworks.

Gone are the severe dress-code rules and strictly limited public galleries. "It's much more relaxed now and the public galleries reflect South African society," says Sisulu. Toyi-toying[6] demonstrations outside the office of the speaker or the chief whip, once inconceivable, are now as commonplace as trade union meetings.

In the bad old days, legislation was more often than not simply rubber-stamped on the cabinet's orders. Now, more than 50 committees work in the full glare of the public eye, open hearings are held on legislation, an all-party rules committee deliberates on how Parliament should be run, and it is not unusual for draft bills to be sent back to ministers for improving.

But besides being a more open and friendly environment, Parliament is rapidly becoming far more efficient and productive than in the past. By the end of the next week, it will have passed 125 bills in 1998, more than double the number passed during that difficult first year and considerably more than were passed annually in the old dispensation.

There are, of course, still problems aplenty - not least in the implementation of all this legislation. There is still a mad rush at the end of each parliamentary session to force through bills that could have been considered at a more leisurely pace.

That has led, in the recent case of the Tobacco Advertising Amendment Bill, to complaints that the public has been heard but not listened to. Eighty submissions were heard on the bill in only two days, leaving many feeling disgruntled that their opinions had been instantly discarded. "We will be using the time between sessions to streamline the process so that bills are ready earlier," says Sisulu.

There are also plans for more thorough public consultations during the policy draft, or green paper, stage of legislation rather than only once bills have reached the committees.

There are also constant bottlenecks, with the understaffed law advisers in Parliament, who must approve and certify every bill, unable to keep up with the

[6] A toyi-toyi is a dance used in political protests

flow. Ideas being bandied about include the co-option of retired lawyers and non-governmental organisations to assist and the "clustering" of similar bills.

"There will always be complaints about things being rushed," concedes Sisulu. "But there are too many bills, all of them important, and there will always be competition for time and space."

Four years on, radical signs of transformation in Parliament are discernible everywhere from the process and people to the artwork. Manuals are even being prepared for the class of '99 to prevent the chaos of '94.

34 EBRAHIM RASOOL: THE ROLE OF MUSLIMS IN THE STRUGGLE

January 24 1999

The words are there for all to see, spray painted on crumbling walls scattered around Athlone: "Kill Ebrahim Rasool".

The graffiti campaign against the ANC's Western Cape chairperson is just another symbol of the tension and violence blistering the social fabric of Cape Town.

It is symptomatic, too, of an environment that has pitted vigilante against gangster, criminal against police officer and citizen against citizen in a spiralling, exasperating wave of death and intimidation.

"My wife and seven-year-old daughter went shopping recently in Athlone and came to a wall that said "Kill Ebrahim Rasool", says the 36-year-old leader of the opposition in the Western Cape legislature.

"My wife drove quickly by. Two hours later my daughter asked, 'Mummy, why do some people want to kill Daddy?'"

Rasool has many such tales. Gone are the days when, even as a provincial cabinet member, he refused to have security personnel guard his home and family. Now, they are part of political life in the Western Cape.

"We have had to change our lifestyle," he says. "Suddenly we live a bit more of a secure life."

Even as the state prepares to throw millions of rands at stemming the tide of crime in the province through Operation Good Hope, Rasool is under no illusion that the divisions run deep and that a radical shift of mindset will be required to restore peace and stability to the troubled Western Cape.

"This last festive season has been one of the bloodiest. The violence, with its threat of ungovernability, is seen as a challenge to the very democratic foundations of our society," he says.

Rasool was born in District Six in 1962 and since his family was forcibly removed to Mannenberg 10 years later, his life has been inextricably linked to the complex political, racial, and religious dynamics of the Western Cape.

At high school he fell under the influence of his principal, Richard Dudley, who was then the president of the black consciousness-aligned New Unity Movement.

While this was an important and informative period, Rasool found the movement's politics too theoretical, too debate oriented and rooted in the coloured middle-class.

This became increasingly evident in the early 1980s when the movement discouraged students from taking part in school boycotts or in campaigning against the creation of the apartheid South African Indian Council.

"The leaders of the Unity Movement were reluctant to have us participate in the boycotts, they had a theoretical approach to the struggle. They argued that the right conditions had to click together in order for there to be a revolution."

Perhaps the event that made him switch his allegiance was a mass rally at Athlone stadium addressed by ANC member Albertina Sisulu, which he attended.

"I suddenly understood that black South Africans were central to any political campaign. Here was song and dance where at Unity Movement meetings there was only debate. There was energy and we almost believed in the inevitability of success."

An important part of Rasool's conversion to the congress movement was the role of Muslims in the struggle, which has given rise to a complex debate and continues to haunt and divide the Cape's Muslim community.

The Iranian revolution in 1979 inspired a radical rethink of Muslim politics, not least of all in the Cape. The notion of an Islamic state was an achievable goal. A host of new organisations sprang up, including the Muslim Students' Association (MSA), which Rasool joined.

"The contradictions emerged when the MSA couldn't define a role for Muslims in the anti-apartheid struggle," he says.

In 1984, disappointed with the MSA's attitude to then President PW Botha's introduction of the tricameral constitution, Rasool and a small band of like-minded thinkers, such as Farid Essak, established the Call of Islam.

Unlike the MSA, Call of Islam became affiliated to the United Democratic Front, of which Rasool was also an executive member.

"I have always been deeply into Muslim politics and I remain in touch. It's part of who I am."

Rasool says that the "onset of modernity" has divided South Africa's Muslim community into three factions.

One is the traditional conservative group, mainly represented by the clergy, who believe Islam is an individual and personal commitment, involving a spiritual, pious life.

He calls another the revivalists. They brook no compromise with modernity, arguing, instead for its replacement by an Islamic state in line with the Iranian revolution.

The third group, of which he considers himself a part, are the progressive post-modernists. "We don't wish modernity away. We find responses that allow you to be a Muslim but also allow you to make a contribution to the world."

The ferocity of disagreement between the groups became evident last month when Rasool had to cancel an address on the topic of Muslims and the African renaissance at an Athlone mosque.

"Pagad [People against Gangsterism and Drugs] and others threatened us with the disruption of the programme if it was not called off. We decided to abandon it, mainly on security grounds," Rasool says.

The intimidation caused rancour in the higher echelons of the ANC. In his address marking the party's 87th birthday, Deputy President criticised both vigilantes and those unwilling to allow freedom of speech.

"There has been a collapse of democratic space in the Western Cape," says Rasool. "It has been subverted by force and by violence."

Earlier this week, Mbeki addressed Muslims in Cape Town. "Many leading activists in our struggle against apartheid were Muslims," Mbeki said. "They did not fight for freedom of expression for another group to emerge with guns and bombs to attack anyone who disagrees with them," he said.

Says Rasool: "Mbeki was arguing that the democratic space needs to be reasserted and he reminded Muslims of their place in South Africa and of their value to society."

However, there is little doubt that Rasool has become one of the main sources of disenchantment for radical Muslims. Late last year he and his family stumbled on to a Pagad braai in Newlands Forest. "Kill political gangsters," they shouted at him.

"Pagad is particularly targeting me," he says. "They hold me responsible for the drastic decline in their support and claim I have divided the Muslim community against them. A few years ago, 30,000 people attended Pagad protests. Now, only a few hundred turn up. We've reached our limit in dealing with Pagad."

As well as religious differences, the fluidity of Cape politics is also marked by a racial dimension.

"The traditional debate between the Africans and the coloureds has been plaguing the ANC for a long time," says Rasool. "Because of the interests of the two communities, they are not easy to reconcile. This has been exploited by the National Party's *swart gevaar* tactics. The NP stampeded people into their camp in 1994, playing on their fears. But since then, the NP haven't delivered."

The coloured community, argues Rasool, is going through an intense period of apathy and cynicism at present.

"At this point, they are like the Israelites who have been led out of Egypt by Moses. Some are still hankering after the fixed identity they were given under apartheid, and they have a fear of what the promised land is all about."

In a bid to accommodate divergent Muslim attitudes as well as embrace coloureds and Africans, Rasool put together a strategy document in April last year for adoption at the party's provincial congress. "The document said, 'listen, we're all poor. Why are we fighting amongst ourselves when white privilege remains untested? We say to whites, 'unless you show generosity, our mutual security will be threatened'."

It is on this basis that the ANC is hoping to capture the lion's share of the votes in the election later this year.

Tensions still exist, admits Rasool, but there is less hostility now.

"With hard work and humility, we need to show that the ANC is not trying to be a party for all seasons but one that is grappling honestly with the contradictions of the Western Cape," he says.

35 THE BANTU HOLOMISA ROAD SHOW

March 14 1999

If General Bantu Holomisa, the United Democratic Movement (UDM) leader, had visited the Cape a couple of weeks ago at a more tranquil moment, his visit in all likelihood would scarcely have been noticed.

Instead, following the death of four party members in the past few days, Holomisa's tour of the impoverished shackland known as KTC had all the markings of a presidential review. A vast convoy of cars teeming with television camera crews, radio and print reporters, photographers from the world's major news agencies and UDM staffers trailed after the general.

At times, some of the cars at the back of the convoy, or the odd latecomer, would lose their way. Locals watched with astonishment as they drove back and forth looking for the general and his entourage. Cars and kombis would do u-turns and speed off down another road, sometimes passing each other at speed, sometimes slowing to exchange information and directions.

When Holomisa stopped at a small brick house to visit Nomonde Xintolo, one widow of the assassinated UDM leader, Ntsikana Ngqwata, the convoy ground to a halt. Two dozen photographers crammed into Xintolo's lounge.

Holomisa's attempt to console the grieving widow was punctuated by the flash and whirr of cameras, the ringing of mobile phones and pagers and the elbowing, seething mass of the media pushing for a better view.

If any of the resident of KTC had been in any doubt as to the importance of Holomisa, or were sceptical about his party's chances of securing the majority in the June election, their fears were surely assuaged.

What minor politician could possibly have attracted such a following? With such a hubbub of activity wherever he went, of course Holomisa was a major force in South African politics. He had, after all, just met Mark Wiley, the Western Cape's provincial community safety minister, and senior police officials.

It was little wonder that when Holomisa arrived to give a speech at the Zolani community centre, at least 400 people packed into the hall to hear his words of wisdom. I suspect the turnout had more to do with careering media convoy than the few hundred pamphlets handed out that morning, or the dark-blue jalopy with loudspeakers on the roof that drove around announcing the show.

Inside the hall, a UDM poster had been hunger over the backdrop for a contest entitled Miss Summer 1998.

The ANC, Holomisa told the crowd, always seemed to be involving itself in political violence, whether in KwaZulu-Natal or the Western Cape: "They are always the common denominator".

Holomisa lashed out at the Independent Electoral Commission, accusing it of pro-ANC bias, rejected the registration "fiasco" and said the government lacked the moral fortitude to stem corruption or violence. "We should not be deceived," he said of the ANC, "by the secret tongues of tyrants." Hardly the stuff of rapprochement, but the crowd loved it. He did, however, urge his followers to show "caution and restraint", and warned that if the UDM did not communicate on the ground with the ANC, "we will perish".

Of course, the death of five people is another tragic chapter in the history of contemporary South Africa. But I couldn't help thinking that in KTC, the deaths served as a major electoral opportunity. The Holomisa roadshow undoubtedly added weight to the general's image, attracting local and international interest.

Bad publicity? No such thing.

36 JOE SEREMANE: 'I WANT TO BREAK THE STEREOTYPES'

March 7 1999

In 1977, Joe Seremane heard God speak. God did not tell Seremane to join the Democratic Party. That happened much later and was not the result of an epiphany.

In 1977, God spoke to Seremane while he was being tortured by the security branch. He was strung up between two chairs in what was called "the helicopter". He had electrodes attached to his body and a gag forced into his mouth. Water was being pumped up his nostrils. He was being beaten.

"I had already given up. I could feel that I was dying," he says. "It gave me a funny satisfaction to know that, in spite of the pain, my life was well given, that maybe others would be inspired when they saw the newspaper headline, 'Joe is dead'."

But, as Seremane contemplated the ebbing away of his life, something began to bother him. His body would be laid to rest in a dark grave and there was no terror in that.

But what of his soul? For the first time since he had abandoned the racially ordered Anglican church of the 1950s ("They told us that is your church but you can't go in, you must worship over there. I never did see the inside of the white church"). Seremane allowed himself a little prayer. He asked God to keep his soul.

"I hard a soft voice. It said: 'I have created this life and, this life that is you, they are not going to take away'."

As the voice stopped, the pain subsided. The torture was halted and Seremane was taken back to serve the rest of his 18-month detention in the solitary confinement to which had become accustomed.

The story is not one that Seremane recounts easily or glibly. It is not described in vivid detail to give him the benefit of some holy endorsement or to endear or enrage those would seek to reject him. It is just a story of one of those moments in life that leads to other moments that lead to the present.

The present is in a bare, fifth-storey office in the Marks building opposite parliament. The papers that are the lifeblood of the legislature have already collected on his desk. It was only last month that Seremane was sworn in as the DP's newest MP in the national council of provinces. He is 61 now and his path here has been long and, at times, difficult.

He was born in August 1938, and grew up with his five brothers and two sisters in the mining town of Randfontein, west of Johannesburg. His father was a miner, his mother a wise but humble domestic worker.

Whites in the town were a constant source of harassment and pain. He remembers being chased frequently by a man on a horse who bore down with a whip on any black person he could find.

On Sunday mornings, town was a place to avoid. No sooner had the white folk left the line of churches that run along main street, still dressed in their Sunday best, than they were pushing blacks off pavements, assaulting and cursing as they went.

"What kind of people are these?" he asked himself.

Safer than town was the rubbish dump on the outskirts where he and his friends spent hours digging around, not for food or broken toys, but for books.

"We'd take them, clean them up and we would exchange them, like a little library. Our favourites were the classics and *Prince Valiant.*"

Frustrated by local hatred and inspired by the new radicalism of the Africanist movement, Seremane left the then docile ANC Youth League of the early 1950s and joined the Pan Africanist Congress.

"For the first time, there was a voice in the African community saying there was no way we could get over our problems by merely non-violent action. There had to be physical, military engagement."

In 1952, at the age of 14, Seremane and his friends were caught up in the fervour of the defiance campaign. Wanting to do their bit, they marched off to the local post office and took their place in the queue on the "white" side.

Asked what they wanted, they replied in raised voices and with the attendant thumb-up salute: "This country is ours. Mayibuye iAfrika!"

"There we were, a group of filthy little boys from the township shouting 'Mayibuye'. Soon we heard the screeching of tyres as the police arrived.

"They grabbed us, caned us and sent us away. Then we went to the railway station and started writing slogans on the subway walls like 'down with segregation'."

Having trained as a teacher, Seremane was arrested after the PAC was banned in 1960s and was sent to Robben Island. He spent seven years in prison from 1963 to 1969. On his release, he was served a banning order and was confined to the magisterial district of Mafikeng.

There he worked for short periods in different jobs. Each time he was hired, the security branch visited his employers and harassed them until he was fired once more. He was arrested again in 1976, just before the Soweto uprising, which he heard about only in December 1977, and was kept incommunicado and tortured repeatedly until 1978,

After his release from jail, and only shortly after he had heard God, Seremane was offered a job as a field worker by the council of churches.

He had also been offered a much better-paying job with Jet Stores, but felt he now owed the church something, particularly if it was non-sectarian and spoke of liberation theology rather than the religion of separation and docility.

"I felt I wanted to say thanks to God," he says of the decision. His politics, like his religion, had also moved into a non-partisan realm.

"I wanted to stand for human rights. I didn't want to be identified with any one particular organisation.

"There are many heroes of the struggle, and they don't all come from one party. They gave their sweat and blood for liberation, and we need to take cognisance of all their contributions."

He quickly proved himself, visiting communities and the homelands to find out how the council of churches could help.

After working for some time as the council's head national field worker in Johannesburg - and narrowly escaping death when the council's headquarters at Khotso House were destroyed by a police bomb in the late 1980s - Seremane was appointed land claims commissioner.

He was unceremoniously sacked by Derek Hanekom, the land affairs minister, last year. The details of that are still sub judice but Seremane claims the accusations of incompetence were the result of "internal politicking" rather than administrative frailty.

"People ask me: 'So why the DP? They're all white, Jewish and rich," Seremane says, lightly toying with his greying goatee beard.

"I want to break the stereotypes. If they are racist or protectionist, I'll tackle this and confront them. I looked at all the leaders of all the parties in 1991 and decided that the DP was a home for visionaries that could one day become a force to be reckoned with. I started addressing DP meetings in the North West.

"In 1994, there was no doubt the ANC was going to win. I wanted them to win, but not completely. Absolute power corrupts absolutely. A good opposition draws the best out of the ruling party.

"Opposition politics is not anti-progressive, or sinister. It makes democracy more resilient. I voted DP in 1994 and did not hide it. I wanted people to think about it. We need a strong opposition to make democracy real."

Adding to his determination not to support the ANC was the death of his brother, Timothy, at Quattro, the ANC's detention camp in Angola. He alluded to his loss in a deeply critical and emotional speech in parliament last week on the topic of the Truth and Reconciliation Commission report.

"Life is precious, no matter who's it is," he told the national assembly, berating the ANC for its lack of disclosure about those who were "murdered in the ANC camps."

But, as his torturer observed back in the late 1970s, in a confession in which he admitted to praying for him each night with his wife, Seremane bears no hate.

"I hate you," Seremane told the torturer.

"No, you don't," the torturer replied. "You say you do, but inside you don't hate." He was right.

37 FRENE GINWALA: 'WELCOME TO MY DUNGEON'

January 31 1999

Deep below parliament's rambling corridors and mahogany panelled committee rooms, there's a prison cell. And while most of those who work in parliament know about it, few have seen the room that Frene Ginwale, the Speaker, calls her 'dungeon'. Fewer yet have been locked up in it, though over the past five years Ginwala must have been tempted on a number of occasions to do just that.

A weekend in the dungeon might have been fitting punishment for the two MPs who engaged in a "bar room" brawl last year on the floor of the national assembly.

The dungeon is a vestige of the Victorian era, which, like the buildings and traditions of the old assembly itself, continues to affect political life in South Africa, even now, at the turn of millennium.

According to the rules that still govern parliament, Ginwala is entitled to make use of the prison cell and can lock up anybody "for a period ending not later that the last day of the then current session". Previously, when parliamentary sessions lasted only six months, that was not too severe. These days, parliament meets for much of the year, making a prolonged stint in the dungeon a rather more uncomfortable prospect.

According to the Powers and Privileges of Parliament Act, MPs and outsiders can be imprisoned if they are found guilty of contempt and do not immediately pay the relevant fine or submit to the deemed punishment. There is no recourse to law. Parliamentary privilege means the courts are not allowed to intervene in internal parliamentary affairs. There is no need for a telephone or lawyers - there's no appeal, or even requirement that you be fed regularly. Quite simply, you can be made to sit there until the last day of the session. If you were thrown into the dungeon today (January 31), you could expect to get out on April 27.

Of course, this has not happened yet, and nor is it likely to. As Ginwala says, with no trace of regret: "I am the only one round here to have a dungeon, but I can't put anybody in it."

The law is useless, or at least that aspect of it. It is, after all, contrary to the constitution, which requires a fair hearing, and the Bill of Rights, which forbids cruel and unusual treatment.

But the law remains on the statute books. The act itself was passed in 1963 and was based on procedures found in the British House of Commons in 1902. However, its principles go even further back to when the British parliament fought a war against the monarchy in the 1640s and the speaker could be beheaded for the slightest infraction. (A mouthwatering prospect for the opposition, perhaps?)

In a recent report to Ginwala, a group of consultants remark - seriously and perhaps rightly - that "the deprivation of liberty is a serious inroad into the rights of the individual ... Whether or not parliament's power to imprison will be considered to be constitutional, the process necessary to imprison will be a burden on parliament while probably also being very damaging to the public perception of parliament". Quite.

The report adds that "the power by parliament itself to imprison for contempt is not widely shared by other parliaments across the world. Successive reports from Britain, where the practice originated, have recommended that it be "abolished". And so it should.

Along with the rule about imprisonment, a number of other oddities, equally outdated, also exist within the act.

MPs, for instance, may not be impeded on their way to work. Technically this could mean that being responsible for a traffic jam could land you in dungeon while MPs could ignore all traffic regulations as being impediments to their access to work for the common good.

Also MPs are at liberty to perform "criminal acts" in parliament and would be immune from prosecution so long as those acts were committed as "part of the proceedings of parliament".

Proving such an act was part of proceedings, however, would probably be a little tricky. I can just see an impoverished backbencher rising with a loaded AK-47 to say: "Madam Speaker, on a point of order I would like to ask all cabinet ministers to empty their pockets." In terms of the law, perfectly justifiable.

In terms of the same law, MPs - or anybody working in parliament - could refuse to stand trial for any civil offence, or give evidence in any such case, in any court outside Cape Town.

The law says clearly that there can be "no civil proceedings in which a member or officer may be brought to trial in a place outside the seat of parliament while that member or officer is in attendance on parliament".

Again, now that the parliamentary sessions last the entire year, more than 1,000 people, of whom only half are MPs, are de jure, if not de facto, exempt from trial.

Such are the imperial foundations on which the laws of our new democratic state are still based. Obviously, they need to be changed.

But five years after the introduction of democracy, we still have a way to go.

38 TONY LEON NEEDS YOU

February 14 1999

On at least a dozen occasions in the past year or two, MPs have been forced to stand up in the national assembly and retract comments in which liken their political opponents to animals. It is accepted practice these days that these remarks are "unparliamentary" - particularly if dogs, pigs or turkeys are the chosen benchmark.

However, the temptation to resort to beastly metaphors often proves too much for MPs to resist. This was evident this week on no less an occasion than the debate on President Nelson Mandela's final opening of Parliament address.

Undeterred by the import of the moment, or by repeated instructions to refrain, animal fever once more seized the high ground of South African political oratory.

Surprisingly, the first culprit was none other than Kader Asmal, the erudite minister of water affairs and forestry.

"The unsuspecting motorist or pedestrian will have noticed a startling sight," Asmal began, warming to his task, the hint of a smile teasing his lower lip. "A political leader's face hanging, bat-like, from our lamp posts. He's our own urban scarecrow, a new traffic hazard, bearer of an urban legend, the understatement of the year: "Tony Leon needs you". His need of support is overwhelming. But what need have we of him and his party?"

However, Asmal's likening of Leon to a bat went unnoticed in the flurry of flowery invective and no retraction was called for.

The same was not true for ANC MP Johnny de Lange, the same political slugger who dropped a National Party member with a roundhouse right after a debate last year. On hearing an interjection from Leon during his speech, De Lange said: "Hua, hua, hua, chihuahua, carry on!"

At this point, Democratic Party MP Douglas Gibson complained: "Madam speaker, my attention has been drawn to the fact that the honourable member referred to another honourable member of this house as a chihuahua. There are repeated rulings in this house that it is unparliamentary for honourable members to compare each other to animals. It's unparliamentary to talk about bullfrogs, apes, baboons, dogs and so on. I ask you to rule that the honourable member withdraw and refer to other honourable members in respectful terms."

The deputy speaker: "Order! Yes, honourable member. You do not need to make a long speech. Honourable de Lange, could you please withdraw that?"

De Lange: "Madam speaker, I withdraw the word 'chihuahua' but I must say that it's an insult more to the chihuahua than to the member."

This was all too much for Leon. Grasping for the most offensive label he could find, he referred to De Lange as "the current honourable bullfrog".

But De Lange has shown again and again he's not a man to stand down when a challenge has been issued. "Madam speaker; I withdraw the comment unconditionally. Now I want to explain to honourable members what a chihuahua is.

"A chihuahua is a little dog. Honourable members should that it's a very arrogant, cocky little dog. Very arrogant indeed."

And so the great minds of our new democratic dispensation got to grips with the state of the nation and the challenges ahead in the next millennium.

After his speech, De Lange was called over for a frosty chat with Mandela. De Lange listened intently for some time as Mandela checked off his points with a finger on his big, boxer's right hand. I doubt whether the president approved.

In closing his address on Wednesday, Mandela referred to the bickering and name-calling only in passing. "Of course, as the tenor of the last two days of debate made clear, members are not unmindful of the looming election," Mandela wryly told the national assembly.

Still, I suppose the sudden rash of animal comparisons is understandable in cosmic if not in political terms. In the Chinese calendar it is, after all, the Year of the Sheep.

39 PUBLIC SERVICE MONSTER SUCKS THE LIFE OUF OF SA

February 21 1999

One of the great ironies of this year's budget came when the New National Party attacked the government for the massive burden public sector salaries are placing on the fiscus.

In his reaction to the speech by Trevor Manuel, the finance minister, Theo Alant, the NNP finance spokesman, called on the government to stop running the public sector "as an employment agency of the ruling alliance."

The NNP's capacity for selective amnesia is staggering. It wasn't that long ago that South Africa had different administrations for whites, coloureds, Indians and blacks, for four provinces and more than half a dozen homelands. The corruption, abuse of public funds, ghostly host of absent workers and duplication still endemic in the public service has very clear origins - and they are not within the past five years.

The public service was run as an employment agency of the ruling alliance from 1948 onward when the sector was used as a solution to the "poor white problem" then considered so hazardous to social stability.

On top of that, the infamous "sunset clause" in the interim constitution forbade the government from ditching public servants in the interests of continuing administration, while a two-year moratorium on retrenchments continues to tie the government's hands.

The audacity of blaming the government for something the NNP created and entrenched over 40 years is astonishing.

Beneath the fickle opportunism, however, lurks a very real problem that will provide Thabo Mbeki with an extremely tough challenge early in his term as president.

The public service has grown out of control. It is sucking the lifeblood out of the economy, limiting spending on job creation, the criminal justice system and social services, and is dampening the prospects for growth.

Even in the muted terms of Manuel's budget speech, the stark facts of what a monster the public service has become, were horribly evident. The public sector wage bill is expected to consume more than half the money - about R83-billion - that the government has available for spending on improving the lives of its citizens this year.

Each year, personnel costs rise at almost the inflation rate, or just more than 12 percent a year. "We cannot afford rising wage costs and improve the quality of services rendered and maintain the current size of the public service," Manuel said.

"The further restructuring of the public service in line with the needs and requirements of our country and our development programme is now urgent ... something has to give."

But thanks in part to the government's new labour laws, the monster that is the public service faces legislation with real teeth. The Labour Relations Act forces the government to consider alternatives to retrenchment, such as redeployment and retraining.

An added difficulty is that, at this stage, the government has no idea of who it should try to retrench, or how many, because it has not yet completed an audit of personnel and skills.

The government will also need to reassess its policy on retrenchment packages, which are generous to say the least. But things are happening. The audit is underway and due to be completed soon. The moratorium on public sector retrenchments expires in July.

The government is becoming increasingly desperate, as is evident through its ever harsher language and firmer attitude. A showdown is looming.

And it is a showdown from which the government, and Mbeki in particular, cannot and should not back away. The next minister of public service and administration, even if Zola Skweyiya keeps the job, will inherit a tinderbox of vested interests, and will have the muscle to shut down government if angered.

The monster that is the public service needs to be put to the sword. To do so will require courage and a steely determination, but it must be done, and it must be done soon.

South Africa cannot afford to spend half its money on government perks and salaries. Mbeki knows it. Manuel knows it and, if they were bold enough to admit it, the public service unions know it. The freeloaders, absentee officials, idle pen-pushers and the corrupt must be forced to leave.

The time has come to uproot the nettle that is strangling the economy.

40 MANDELA'S DREAM OF RECONCILIATION PROVES ELUSIVE

February 28 1999

Perhaps it was overly optimistic of President Nelson Mandela to hope that national reconciliation could be achieved in five years.

From the evidence of the special parliamentary debate on the Truth and Reconciliation Commission on Thursday night, we have a long, long way to go.

Bitterness, sorrow and anger simmer beneath the South African body politic.

Listen to the voices: the commission is a "sensationalist circus of horrors presided over by a weeping clown" (Mangaqa Mncwango, Inkatha Freedom Party); "The entire white political establishment ... has blood on its hands" (Peter Mokaba, ANC): "I have never felt so humiliated ... this is suppression of a minority group" (Constand Viljoen, Freedom Front); "In war, there's no neutrality in silence" (Mac Maharaj, ANC); "*Thula* (shut up), tsotsi comrades" (Joe Seremane, Democratic Party).

How flimsy our democracy appears against such a deep and turbulent divide.

Is there a way out? Can we ever really move on from apartheid? Do not be deluded that the answers are a given; that our stroll to peace, prosperity and unity is inevitable. The future hangs in the balance.

This week's debate illustrated a fundamental point: that the completion of the truth commission's work is the beginning, and not the conclusion, of the quest for national reconciliation.

The reality is that five years of intense self-contemplation has been nowhere near enough.

The ANC is angry that its freedom struggle has been equated with the defence of apartheid. The IFP is angry that the truth about its own struggle has not been exposed. The Freedom Front and Democratic Party are angry the entire white community, and Afrikaners in particular, are still blamed.

Victims are angry that they have not heard the whole truth and will not receive adequate compensation. Perpetrators are angry that they have been abandoned by their leaders.

There's a lot of anger, from nearly every corner of society. On top of this, the inequality in income, opportunities and quality of life petrified during the long, dark years of colonialism and apartheid - remain as immutable as Table Mountain.

"The incontestable fact," Deputy President Thabo Mbeki said in a powerful speech, "is that in many respects ours remains, still, an apartheid society."

But what is to be done? For guidance we turn to Mandela. Reconciliation, in many ways, is his child and his gift. Though his long walk is a stiff shuffle these days, his vision is clear.

"The quest for reconciliation was the fundamental objective of the people's struggle," he told a packed Parliament.

It "was the spur that gave life to our difficult negotiation process and the agreements that emerged from it. The search for a nation at peace with itself is the primary motivation for our Reconstruction and Development Programme, to build a better life for all ."

As to the future, there were four key requirements: build a strong human rights culture to prevent such abuse from happening again; pursue, extradite, and prosecute - within a time limit - those who have not accounted for apartheid atrocities; heal and rehabilitate the wounded; and mobilise resources, the government and the private sector to exhume and bury the dead and to help the victims.

41 THE END OF THE MANDELA ERA

March 07 1999.

And so South Africa's first democratic Parliament has risen for the last time and the Mandela presidency nears its end.

Yes, there are two more months of goodbyes with speeches and tributes aplenty to come. A good deal will also be said on the hustings. But the business is done and it is for history - and the electorate - to judge the merits and import of these past five years.

There will never again be a period in South Africa quite like this one.

Future generations will read aghast of the lunacy of apartheid and of the long struggle to overturn it.

They will hear of this Parliament churning out more than 500 pieces of legislation in a desperate bid to clear the statute books of the prejudices of the past and fill them with the rights and hopes of the future.

They will look with disbelief at the crime statistics, at the horrible impact of the HIV-Aids epidemic and at the ubiquity of corruption. They will see that decades of injustice are a sure recipe for moral degeneration, self-interest, violence, and hatred and that these things take years to turn around.

Few, however, even among the opposition benches, would deny that in the last five years significant strides have been made to put South Africa on its feet again. First and foremost, we are a country at peace.

There is no talk of armed insurrection nor of civil war. There is little likelihood of racial conflagration nor of ethnic mobilisation. There is no army of rightwingers waiting in the wings to seize part of South Africa.

Millions more people now have access to water, electricity and housing, health care, welfare and the dignity of human rights.

Overall, though, the name of Mandela will be writ large.

Though liberation was never the work of one man, Mandela's presence will forever be associated with the transition from tyranny to justice.

With Mandela gone and apartheid a fading memory, we become something we scarcely dreamed possible even a few years ago: a normal country.

This has its own challenges too. We are fortunate that, as a parting gesture, for Mandela, the European Union has finally given the nod to a free trade agreement for South Africa.

But the world is in need of constant convincing that South Africa is worthy of interest and support. We can no longer rely on the name of Mandela or on the victory of liberation to attract foreign investment and finalise trade agreements.

This we will have to do ourselves in a deeply competitive, global environment where, once justice has been secured, stability, growth potential and competitive advantage will become the measures of success.

To ensure these we will - in all likelihood - have to rely on Mandela's successor, Thabo Mbeki.

What the Mandela presidency has begun, the Mbeki administration will be required to give effect to. From the age of the icon, we move now to the era of the manager; from heady symbols and feelgood notions, we move to the bottom line of efficiency.

With much of the old apartheid state will intact, this will be no easy task. With few additional resources available, this will be more difficult yet.

But do it we must and as quickly as possible. We can all, however, look back with pride at the last five years. For we have all played our part in making the miracle.

South Africa's first democratic Parliament has done its job and Mandela's first, and last, presidential term is all but complete.

The rest is up to us.

42 THABO MBEKI: THE KING OF CHARM

September 1 1995

The pipe smoke still lingers in the air as Thabo Mbeki walks across the deep-pile carpet of his expansive Tuynhuys office, hand outstretched. The Man Who Will Be President doesn't smoke much in public these days. His close ally, Health Minister Nkosazana Zuma, has seen to that.

Ironically, Mbeki is just like the FW De Klerk of old: when the Press are around, the smokes are hidden away. But the perfumed smell is as unmistakable as the affable smile, the warm handshake, the first-name familiarity.

For Mbeki, charm is part of the package. It has marked his career as distinctively as his predecessor's personality was forged by years on Robben Island. It has seen him converse as comfortably with peasants as with kings, with Afrikaners as with Zulus.

It is difficult not to respond positively when presented to Mbeki. He is always immaculately dressed and reassuringly relaxed, and his love of language means an errant word or inappropriate epithet is never allowed to slip from his lips. Pedantic to the point of obsession - he jokingly calls it "my disease" - Mbeki insists on every subordinate clause being put in its proper place, and every word performing its duty in the way nature intended.

He abhors ambiguity, hyperbole, imprecision. All political considerations aside, it is somehow comforting to know that we will have at our helm a man who knows exactly where the apostrophe does not go in the possessive form of "its".

But it is not just language about which Mbeki is fastidious. He is equally concerned about ideas. He wonders aloud whether capitalism perpetuates its own value system of wealth accumulation, as argued by George Soros. He quotes Gogol, the 19th Century Russian writer, on the notion of "dead souls" and hopelessness. He grapples with the ways in which society can be measured and improved.

These are concepts one would expect to be mulled over by a philosophy don, not a politician with an election to run, another meeting to rush to, another crisis to control. When people speak of Mbeki's intellectualism, though, they are not necessarily referring to his ability to namedrop, nor to pepper his speeches with classical references, nor even to engage those paid or willing to listen to questions of political philosophy.

They do so because Mbeki, unlike Mandela, will argue a point through until he has it straight. Cabinet ministers who got away with a pat on the back and a "we know you're trying" under Mandela face a far more stringent examination of their progress under Mbeki. The charismatic icon is being replaced with the manager, the symbol of reconciliation with the interrogator.

Few would argue that the change is not for the good. Now that the miracle has been achieved, South Africa requires someone with the willingness and the capacity to make it work. But will reconciliation, in particular toward white South Africans, also be lost when Mandela goes?

Despite the dinner-party perception that he is a man who harbours a deep strain of bitterness towards his white compatriots, Mbeki's notion of Africanism is a broad an all-encompassing one. It was Mbeki who was the first among the ANC's exiled leaders to reach out to the Afrikaner.

Quite simply, this is a man who does not suffer fools gladly, be they black or white. He has lashed out at young blacks for their "culture of entitlement", and at black teachers for arriving at school drunk, just as he has criticised whites for their inherent sense of superiority and their apparent inaction in the face of poverty and injustice.

The distinction in style and personality between Mbeki and Mandela has added an extra dimension to the notion that Mbeki is distant, unapproachable, even unfathomable.

Indeed, so little is known about Mbeki, about his life and preferences, about his friends and habits, that more often than not, the worst is assumed. That is not that surprising, given that Mbeki has spent most of his adult life outside South Africa, working within an organisation that was by nature clandestine and a touch paranoid.

The habits of a lifetime are not easily shrugged off. Often it is those he most trusts that Mbeki rewards, regardless of their intellect or ability. It is for this reason that the Pahad brothers, Aziz and Essop, are amongst his closest circle of advisors and friends. Through the hard years of exile, when, for instance, he was criticised for being too liberal due to his education at the "western" University of Sussex, they stood by his side.

Even those closest to Mbeki worry that they have never really known him. Some would say that it is simply not possible to look behind the large, black pupils and blue-specked irises and see the real Thabo Mbeki. But sitting here in his office, fresh from another jousting session with the ANC's parliamentary caucus, he is friendly and articulate.

Not much can be assumed from the décor, which is functionally pleasant. An ornate, Ghanaian ebony chair has pride of place, the gift of a trade delegation. A crystal paperweight sits isolated on a half-acre of empty desk. There are no piles of paper in the in-tray or the out-tray. Behind the desk a large coat of arms hangs on the wall beside a certificate of Outstanding Leadership presented to him by Mandela in 1995. Local landscapes in light pastels are dotted around at intervals.

"What's wrong with a flowery head?" he asks a slightly embarrassed photographer who was wondering if a bowl of paper carnations could be moved from the mantelpiece behind the Deputy President.

Mbeki takes no credit for his appearance, though it is always immaculate. "My wife Zanele chooses my suits for me. They're just off-the-rack. I've tried tailors a few times, but they don't seem to work. I had three suits made for me in India but had to give them away. All three were useless".

Mbeki's mother, Epainette, complains that her son's large, plantation-style house in the Cape Town suburb of Newlands is "not very homely". But Mbeki is no ordinary, home-loving man because his has been no ordinary life. It has been a life marked by hardship and loneliness, and much of who he is relates back to who he was.

As Nelson Mandela said in a speech at his daughter Zindzi's wedding: "It seems to be the destiny of freedom fighters to have unstable personal lives".

The family into which Mbeki was born was torn apart and scattered to the winds during the struggle against apartheid. His father, Govan, was imprisoned for almost three decades. His sister was detained on the most spurious of grounds. His youngest brother is missing, presumed killed; his only child, a son, has also disappeared and is presumed dead.

Mbeki himself, after spending much of his childhood in boarding schools and away from home, lived in exile for almost 30 years. As his mother says of him now, "Thabo has paid the price. He really has".

To understand the price, and the impact it has had on him, one has to go back to the beginning, back to a remote and windswept hillside village called Mbewuleni in the Transkei. Here, in 1940, two young newly-weds, Govan Mbeki and Epainette Moerane, settled to begin a life together.

Trained as a teacher, the outspoken Govan was never able to hold down a teaching job for long, thanks to repeated disagreements with one school authority after another - invariably over a political matter. For the most part, he earned a modest living writing articles for newspapers such as The Guardian and New Age.

Mbeki's mother, known to one and all as Ma Mofokeng, ran a small trading store to supplement the family income, and baked cakes and scones for a local coffee shop. These were not easy years for Thabo Mbeki and his siblings. Govan was often absent and, when he was home, was preoccupied with work.

"I never really had time for the children," he confesses. "Not that I didn't like them. Not that I didn't love them. But I was doing writing and reading so I didn't have the time to be playing with them. So I pushed them on to the mother. Come go and play there or get to your mother or leave me alone. So I don't know how they feel today. Probably they feel that I didn't pay sufficient attention to them as children. I wouldn't blame them if they felt like that".

In a sense, Mbeki would come to know his father better from his books and his writing than from their interactions. But the young Mbeki, too, turned out to be a born academic.

At school in Queenstown, where he lived with his uncle, Michael Moerane, Mbeki's brilliance as a scholar soon became apparent to all. He scored first-class grades in all his subjects. As Michael Moerane was a music teacher, Mbeki also learned to play the piano and the flute.

Govan talks fondly of the day that he went to visit and found all six of Moerane's children, along with his son, playing different musical instruments in an ensemble. Years later, as a 14-year-old matric student at Lovedale College in Alice, Mbeki one day asked his boarding master whether he could have the keys to the piano room.

"But no one has been in there for thirteen years," the teacher replied. When the keys were finally found and the piano unearthed from the cobwebs, it was unplayable. "I would probably be quite good at the piano now if it wasn't for that," rues Mbeki. "The school didn't have the money to fix it".

There is a sadness in Mbeki's eyes as he thinks back to his youth. It is the melancholy of lost opportunities, of enduring solitude and of a commitment, even then, to some grand political notions that most adolescents would rate well down their hierarchy of needs.

He was earnest about his place in the world then; he is earnest now. Mbeki keeps his jacket on throughout the interview, his flat-soled shoes crossed neatly, his silk tie following the contours of his slim form.

No matter how charming and casual the conversation, or how light the laugh and the smile, Mbeki projects an intimidating inner presence: an emotional portcullis ready to drop at the first sign of unwelcome intrusion.

"There was nothing that was right about apartheid," he says almost viciously, enunciating each word. The phrase hangs massively in the silent room. No one will speak or even nod until he releases us from the pause. At last he continues, leading us back to the distant days of his youth.

At Lovedale College, more drama was about to befall the young Mbeki. First, he was expelled for his part in student strikes against the introduction of Bantu Education. Second, he fell in love.

Having girlfriends in the kind of rural setting he grew up in was strictly taboo. It was marriage or nothing. Not his friends, or even his family, knew when he started seeing Olive Nokwanda Mphahlwa, daughter of the local school principal.

Nokwanda was attending school in a nearby village, and she and Mbeki met for a rendezvous beyond the prying eyes of the villagers. The relationship, however, soon developed from the innocence of first love into more intimate contact. Nokwanda was pregnant.

The pregnancy, while not unheard of amongst the young, caused a stir in the village. After a series of behind-closed-doors meetings, it was agreed that the Mbeki family should pay five head of cattle - the usual penalty for making an underage girl pregnant. Mbeki was still only 16.

Kwanda Monwabise, Mbeki's only child, was born in 1959 and lived with his mother and her family for 10 years. He was then taken into the Mbeki kraal and stayed with Ma Mofokeng until he passed his matric.

Mbeki saw Kwanda for the last time when he was only a toddler, two years old. In 1961, Mbeki left for post-matric studies in Johannesburg and a year later had left the country altogether for exile. He would only return home almost three decades later. By that time, Kwanda had disappeared, presumed killed by the apartheid security forces.

Mbeki's youngest brother, Jama, also disappeared. The same fate is believed to have befallen him. Mbeki's sister, Linda, was imprisoned for 10 months on suspicion of working for the ANC. Govan spent 25 years on Robben Island. Mbeki himself went into exile.

The struggle for democracy in South Africa caused untold suffering and loss to the Mbeki family. It splintered them as effectively as a bolt of lightning would a blue-gum tree. These experiences explain, in part, Mbeki's disapproval of the culture of entitlement displayed by the new generation of younger black South Africans, as well as hostility to those who jealousy guard their old privileges without embracing the new order.

"The measure of the success of a society is the state of its most under-privileged citizens," he says.

In exile, Mbeki attended the University of Sussex in England and graduated with a Masters in economics in 1966. It was at this time that he received his first message from his imprisoned father. It was contained in a letter sent from Robben Island to his mother and then relayed to him via the Tambo family in London. Study on, the message said. Get your doctorate.

Mbeki had never asked for advice from his father before, not personal, political or otherwise. But Govan felt that a doctorate would open doors for his son, would win him respect and admiration wherever he went. He felt it so important he broke the unwritten, unspoken contract of a lifetime to convey his wishes.

Govan received no response and did not bother to try again. As he said later: "In my family, no one depends on one another, no one looks to the other for this or the other thing. We work as a team, as I work with my comrades in the ANC. Thabo has never asked for advice. We strengthen ourselves."

Mbeki ignored his father's recommendation. Rather than studying on, he went to work with ANC President Oliver Tambo and Communist Party leader Dr Yusuf Dadoo in the ANC's London office. As he soon learned, life in exile was a very different proposition to studying full-time.

Inside South Africa, the ANC had been crushed and humiliated. Outside, they squabbled over strategy and ideological preference. The movement was a hotbed of insecurity. Into this quagmire, Mbeki stepped gingerly. As a clever, western-educated intellectual, he had to protect his back. Loyalty and trust became vital qualities to Mbeki, as they are now.

It was during his first few years in London that Mbeki fell in love again. This time, the object of his affections was a post-graduate social worker by the name of Zanele Dlamini. In those days, ANC cadres had to ask permission to marry from a party committee. They were, after all, refugees, with no money and their weddings, rings and honeymoons were all paid for out of party coffers. Many a request had been turned down on the grounds that "we did not bring you here to get married".

Mbeki was desperate. He confided in Adelaide Tambo, his virtual mother in exile. "Thabo came to me one day and said, 'Mama, I want to marry Zanele'," recollects Adelaide. "'Well, put in your application and see what happens', I said to him. 'Mama, if Papa (Oliver Tambo) doesn't allow me to marry Zanele, I'll never, ever marry again. And I'll never ask again. I love only one person and there is only one person I want to make my life with, and that is Zanele'. He was very determined to marry her."

Fortunately, the request was approved. But it was to be far from a normal marriage. Zanele was soon off to the United States to complete a doctorate and Mbeki was sent to Swaziland to take control of the ANC's forward bases in the area.

They saw each other from time to time but it was only when Zanele was hired by the United Nations High Commissioner for Refugees and was based in Africa and Mbeki was posted to Nigeria and then to ANC headquarters in Lusaka, Zambia, that they could live together for any extended period of time.

Mbeki spent several years shoring up the ANC's presence in Swaziland, debriefing new exiles, transporting arms and ammunition from Mozambique, engaging in political work and travelling the subcontinent before being sent to Nigeria. In Lagos, he was appointed the ANC's chief representative and began to fashion a new arrow for his quiver.

While the ANC battled to establish a political or military presence in South Africa, and was torn and divided over policy within the exiled leadership, internationally it began to gather prestige as the authentic voice of the South African majority. Much of this was due to the role of a few, well-spoken, intelligent, affable ambassadors. Individuals with Mbeki's gifts became inordinately important.

As head of the ANC's diplomatic mission in Nigeria, Mbeki put his diplomatic skills to the test and impressed African and western leaders alike. Little by little, he was becoming a well-rounded, consummate politician: well connected, well read and highly articulate. His inner pain was covered with an over reasonableness.

The ease with which he conversed with all kinds of people was to push him to the forefront of the ANC's image building, as well as strategic, initiatives. From Lagos, Mbeki was brought back to serve as Tambo's political secretary and then director of information.

As Tambo's speech writer and confidant, he had his fingers on the pulse of the liberation struggle. But it was a struggle that had reached a kind of impasse. The party's military objectives were still bearing little fruit, glasnost in Europe threatened to deprive the liberation movement of resources, and its efforts at political organisation inside South Africa were making painfully slow progress.

At the ANC's Consultative Conference at Kabwe, Zambia, in 1985, the possibility of entering into "talks" with the apartheid government were raised for the first time. After a series of meetings both with Afrikaner intellectuals in Lusaka and Afrikaner business people in Britain, it was Mbeki who led the first ANC delegation to meet with representatives of the South African National Intelligence Service in secret at a hotel in Switzerland in 1989.

The meetings were codenamed Operation Flair and were the first real step toward negotiations surrounding the unbanning of the ANC and the holding of democratic elections.

The better-known part of the Mbeki story unfolded after his return from exile in 1990. Initially over-shadowed by the ANC's secretary-general and chief negotiator Cyril Ramaphosa, he surprised many by securing the deputy presidency in Mandela's first democratic government.

Ramaphosa's departure from the political area, the sidelining of a number of potential competitors such as Tokyo Sexwale, Patrick Lekota and Bantu Holomisa, and the gradual concentration of power in the office of the deputy presidency have fuelled rumours of Mbeki's tendency for manipulation.

But it is with some satisfaction that Mbeki now sits atop the pile of political power in South Africa. He has endured half a century of turmoil and pain, joy and deprivation, isolation and victory. Many of his habits and beliefs remain intact: his high regard for loyalty, his solitude, his work ethic, his reading. And though the struggle has changed, it has new demands that are as consuming as ever.

In the office of the Deputy President at Tuynhuys, we have long over-stayed our allotted time. But Mbeki looks neither restless nor impatient. He never glances at the clock on the wall. It is his aides who start rustling papers.

Finally, his personal assistant can contain herself no longer. "We are late, chief," she says. Mbeki nods his quickly greying head and stands. He shrugs as if to say, "What can I do?", smiles and offers his hand once more. The King of Charm has had his say. His convoy is waiting.

43 FIVE YEARS ON: DEMOCRACY HAS COME A LONG WAY

May 16 1999

It is worth taking a few moments to remember what state South Africa was in about this time five years ago, little more than two weeks before our first democratic election.

The headlines alone, taken from the days leading up to the poll, went like this: "Nine killed as car bomb rocks Jo'burg", "Bomb madness grips SA", "People blown to pieces at (taxi) rank", "Nine die, 92 hurt in car bomb blast", "Blast at IEC offices", "TV disrupted as blasts hit W Tvl towers" and "3 blasts in Free State".

The explosions, the innocent victims, the loss and suffering of survivors, was only a small part of what South Africa was experiencing. You may remember that the Inkatha Freedom Party, right up until April 20 - exactly seven days before the poll - remained outside the process.

Violence between IFP and ANC supporters in KwaZulu-Natal was endemic at the time, resulting in thousands of deaths every year.

People began to hoard tinned foods, petrol and water in anticipation of the worst. Many who could afford to leave the country did so and watched on from somewhere safe.

In addition, we have learnt since those days that the rightwing was ready to launch a civil war: General Constand Viljoen told me recently that he had at his disposal at least 60,000 armed troops ready to defend a white *volkstaat*.

The only thing holding the right-wing back were the conflicting views surrounding where that *volkstaat* should be, along with worries over the lack of discipline displayed by the Afrikaner Weerstandsbeweging both in Bophuthatswana, where an attempted coup was put down by the former homeland's defence force, and at the World Trade Centre, where they drove an armoured vehicle through the front door and urinated in the negotiating council chamber.

More than 200 right-wing extremist groups had been established by 1993, some of which were helping themselves to state munitions in preparation for war. One of the radical groups, the Boere Krisisaksie, raided a military arms depot in November 1993 and stole more than three tons of equipment, including 100,000 rounds of ammunition, 400 handgrenades and 200 mortars.

During January 1994, 30 acts of sabotage were conducted against ANC offices and personnel in the then Western Transvaal and the Free State. Forty-one bombs were set off in the Western Transvaal in the first week of February alone.

Not only was South Africa a mess of violence and death, it teetered on the brink of self-destruction. Little wonder that the world held its breath in expectation of a bloody, racial conflagration.

"This is a war against the whole nation," Tokyo Sexwale, later the Gauteng premier, said at the time. "We will not allow an Angola situation in this country".

Now here we sit, five years later, and our most serious problem seems to be preventing too many potential voters from sleeping through election day.

The closest we have come to a fight this month was when the feuding Rajbansis faced each other at a Mother's Day cultural show in the Indian heartland of Chatsworth. The former couple, whose colourful divorce was widely reported last year, now represent different political parties.

Amichand Rajbansi has lodged a complaint with the Independent Electoral Commission, claiming his wife's signature on the acceptance candidature form (as an IFP candidate) was forged.

"I have submitted a seven-page complaint to the IEC about this alleged fraud. Remember: I was once a no-nonsense soccer referee and administrator of the game and I can spot a forged signature immediately," he huffed. His former wife, Asha Devi, retorted: "This is the biggest load of rubbish in our ongoing dispute. The man is desperate."

In a telling remark on the election campaign, the bureau chief of a well-known international news service spoke ruefully of the apparent lack of interest in South Africa's second democratic poll. "There is not much interest," he said. "South Africa is becoming a normal country".

Normality! For how many years have we desired such an assessment. Now, it's official. Other than a few deaths in Nyanga in the Western Cape some weeks ago, and some trouble in Richmond, South Africa has become, in political terms, a quiet, peaceful, normal place.

Admittedly, there have been reports of poster vandalism and even complaints of the occasional threat or attempt at intimidation, but compared to late March and April 1994, we are in a very different place.

Even the mass defections just before the candidate lists were finalised appear to have had little impact on our lives in five years. For all the current grievances, we have much to celebrate.

The importance of taking part should not be lost on anyone.

44 GERALD MORKEL: 'LIVE AND LET LIVE'

August 12 1999

Western Cape Premier Gerald Morkel waggles his hips and lines up the golf club on his plush office carpet.

He smiles as the shiny, new club - an unusual number-11 wood - sweeps to-and-fro through the deep pile. His aides instinctively stand back a yard or two, for fear their boss will take a full-blooded swing and, in the process, do damage to the chandelier, the mahogany desk or possibly themselves.

Practising with his new clubs in his Wale Street suite is about as close as Morkel gets these days to playing the odd sporadic round.

Since the June election, changes are afoot in the provincial legislature that are likely to see him spend even less time pursuing his favourite hobby amongst the trees and grass of his beloved province.

For the year leading up to the poll, after he had stepped into the shoes of his predecessor Hernus Kriel, Mr Morkel was mainly concerned with "patching cracks", or managing the crisis within the New National Party.

Party members were defecting in droves, an election defeat loomed large and talk of a possible coalition government was already in the air. Endless official engagements crowded his diary like four-balls on a Saturday morning at the Royal Cape golf club.

This left little time for the day-to-day management of the province. Oddly enough, and unlike most other provinces, the old Premier's office was never really geared to this task. Ministers generally did their own thing and the premier's R6-million annual budget and small staff encouraged giving advice and attending functions rather than hands-on involvement in line function duties.

This is all set to change.

The premier now has R17-million allocated to his office for the year. The expanded budget includes provision for communications, the monitoring of cabinet and departmental performance, additional support staff, the incorporation of a director general and the tools to comply with the new Public Administration Act and its demands of greater financial responsibility.

But in a rare moment of peace, Mr Morkel can't resist taking out his new golf club and swinging it in his office.

"I feel like a child, I'm so excited," he says.

Later in the day, his silver Mercedes glides past the waterfall at the entrance to his magnificent residence, Leeuwenhof.

Beyond the palm trees and garden sculptures, the Atlantic glimmers in failing light and the rush-hour roar softens to a distant drone.

"It's a very beautiful place," he says of the 200-year-old home, "but we don't get the time to enjoy it. In the year that I've been here, I've been in the pool once".

Inside Leeuwenhof, stale wood smoke hangs in the air as thickly as the artwork on the walls and the Persian rugs on the stone floor.

There is a large sign saying "Private" on the door of Mr Morkel's favourite room, his study. The sign applies to all, residents and visitors alike.

"I can't get to sleep before 1am so I work until late every night," says Mr Morkel. "There's always so much to do".

Unlike many of the previous occupants of Leeuwenhof, the Morkels are determined to allow the citizens of the Cape to use these lavish premises as a resource. The former slave quarters is now a conference facility and the endless, 50-seater teak table often is host to foreign and local dignitaries.

Five hundred township children recently held a party in Leeuwenhof's ample grounds, one of more than 60 functions hosted by the Morkels in the last year.

"This place belongs to the taxpayers of Cape Town," says Mr Morkel.

"Where we are today, people brought us here," says Mr Morkel's wife of 39 years, Hazel.

Mrs Morkel is deeply involved in community work herself, runs a charity fund and occasionally has to stop her highly-politicised family from continuing their work boisterously at home.

"I have to say 'just stop now, we're at home, just relax'," laughs Mrs Morkel.

Given their hectic schedules, it's a miracle they see each other at all. "We do see each other," says Mrs Morkel, "sometimes, in the passage".

Two of the Morkel's children, Gail, 25, and Craig, 31, stay at home. Craig has recently been elected to the national Parliament while Kent, their oldest child, is the chair of the Cape Metropolitan Council.

"I've really not encouraged them to go into politics," says Mr Morkel. "I've never pushed them but always said 'do what you want to do, only enjoy it'."

The Morkels, however, don't always see eye to eye. Mr Morkel, for instance, is a Manchester United fan while his sons support Liverpool.

Mr Morkel was himself a reluctant entrant into the realm of politics. He was in the building trade in the early 1980s when a business colleague asked whether he could hold a political meeting in the Morkel's Retreat home.

"I said to him 'man, I don't have time for politics', but he said 'please, man, come to the meeting'. So they came to my house and had dinner. They made a lot of sense. They were all Labour Party people, including Allan Hendrickse, and argued that the time had come to have representation at Parliament. They had been in the Coloured Representative Council and the only avenue open to them was the tricameral Parliament. The only other option was revolution and anarchy.

"They wanted to form a branch as Retreat had just become a new constituency. I agreed to give them some money. They said they wanted me in the branch and then said they couldn't go on if I didn't become the chairman of the branch. Every organisation I've ever been in, I've been the chairman. So I said 'alright'. Then they were putting together nomination lists for candidates. 'It's only four days a week, you'll have time to carry on with your business,' they told me. 'Alright,' I said. And it just went on from there. Eventually, being a person who does things seriously, I gave up my business interests and my directorships and went full time into politics".

Since his younger years, Mr Morkel has had one important ruling principle: "Live and let live".

"I was an apprentice builder many years ago and was travelling in the car with my boss. Somebody almost crashed into us and my boss leaned out the window and shouted 'live and let live'. It's been my philosophy throughout my life. It's meaning is that you must be tolerant of others."

Time draws on and the Premier is due at another function. He can't resist, however, taking just one mor look at that new golf club.

45 NELSON MANDELA'S BUSY RETIREMENT

December 9 1999

A new house is being built for Nelson Mandela in his home village of Qunu and a bridge under the nearby highway is awaiting his early morning rambles. But it may be some time yet before he can sit under a tree, play with his grandchildren and watch his cattle fatten in the fields.

For now, South Africa's ambassador plenipotentiary has much more important things to do. Not least of these is no less an objective than bringing peace to the Middle East.

It is an idea that he has mulled over for years.

"This is a matter of interest not only to the people of the Middle East but throughout the world," he said this week after a meeting with representatives of the Cape's Jewish Board of Deputies.

Undeterred by the intractability of the problems, the hardened attitudes and the decades of conflict and mistrust, Mandela has set out on a round of hectic shuttle diplomacy that has seen him criss-crossing the globe for months.

Armed with a three-point proposal, Mr Mandela is in Seattle meeting United States President Bill Clinton this week. In October he visited Israel, Syria, Iran and Jordan. He is in regular contact with British Prime Minister Tony Blair, French President Jacques Chirac and with a range of other leaders from Egypt's Hosni Mubarak to Libya's Muammar Ghadaffi.

Last week a South African delegation led by deputy foreign affairs minister Aziz Pahad was also in the territory following up on the Mandela proposal. They went to Iraq, Lebanon, Kuwait as well as both Syria and Jordan.

"He just feels there is an opportunity to break the logjam," Pahad said this week. "In general, everybody supports him".

The proposal, in essence, is three-fold: Arab states need to recognise Israel as a sovereign country with secure borders, Israel must withdraw from the Golan Heights occupied during the Six Day War in 1967 and an international commission must be set up to oversee the implementation of the new peace accord.

Simple it may seem, but each of these demands calls for major compromises on a range of emotive issues from many of the key players of the troubled region.

Adding to the complexity is the number of other initiatives, not least one spearheaded by the United States secretary of state Madeleine Albright, also currently underway.

Mr Mandela, though, sees no contradiction, no clouding of the waters, in his role.

"There have been a number of initiatives over the years, none of which has succeeded," he points out frankly. "One of the weaknesses has been that each country wants to use the Middle East to build their own interests and not the interests of the people of the Middle East."

Mandela's plan is to combine all the initiatives, past and present, so that "we can all speak with one voice". His idea, though, is that he will act only as the catalyst before leaving the technical details to others: "Once we start to bring all these various initiatives together. I will then leave it to younger people, like Mr

Clinton. This is my aim."

Naturally enough, there has been resistance to the Mandela plan. Neither the Israelis nor the Syrians have officially responded to his suggestions, though both claim they support his role, experience, and moral standing.

Says Ze'ev Luria, an Israeli diplomat based in South Africa: "The visit of former President Mandela to Israel in late October was a significant expression of the government of South Africa to show support in the government and the people of Israel."

"We appreciate his good intentions," said Luria of Mandela. "However, we welcome the policy of the government of South Africa to support the peace process and try to facilitate it without supporting one side or interfering."

Luria added, however, that the "best way" for securing peace in the Middle East was in "direct talks" between Israel and the Palestinians. "It could be undermining to ask for interventions by the international community."

A certain hesitancy is natural enough, given the ANC's long-standing ties with Yasser Arafat and the Palestinians.

Mandela has gone out of his way to bring the South African imperative to consult and brief all parties to bear on his work. On his trip to the Middle East in October, he took two high-ranking members of the local Jewish community, including Chief Rabbi Cyril Harris, along for the ride. He has been meticulous about shoring up relations with Jewish leaders both at home and internationally (he will be meeting American Jewish leaders this week) and has sought to involve them at every opportunity.

Additional signs of willing have included the invitation, extended through President Thabo Mbeki, for Israeli President Ezer Weizman to visit South Africa next year and the growing volume of bilateral trade and closer political ties between the two countries.

The Palestinians, too, seem to be happy with the bringing to bear of Madiba

Magic on the peace process.

Says El Herfi Salman, the ambassador of the state of Palestine, "Nelson Mandela is a friend of the Palestinian people, and he is also looking to be a friend of the Israeli people.

"We welcome his proposal and his initiative, and we have informed him officially of our appreciation. He can give a lot to the peace process in the Middle East especially as it is backed by the very special experience of South Africa."

"He also has the support of other Arab leaders and it is unfortunate that the Israeli side has not agreed to his proposal."

Critics argue, however, that not only has Mandela failed to convince the Israelis of his bona fides, but he has also taken on his role in the Middle East without the backing of either President Mbeki or the support of South Africa's department of foreign affairs.

Mandela gave weight to this recently, perhaps only by omission, by mentioning a whole list of people with whom he had consulted in recent weeks but forgetting to add in President Mbeki. He soon corrected himself once asked directly.

Mr Pahad was quick to set the involvement of his ministry and the presidency straight: "We have had several discussions, four I think... He is in touch with all the role players and is trying to add his voice to get a real breakthrough. We must not underestimate his personal stature in the world. People have to take very seriously what he's saying."

For Pahad, the benefits of a final settlement in the Middle East would provide enormous benefits for South Africa and the world.

"We have important Moslem and Jewish communities in South Africa so of course we are interested in what is happening. The Middle East process will impact on North Africa and us too. Solving those problems will open up tremendous opportunities for broader economic and political relations in that area."

In spite of the obvious difficulties and the arduous nature of the task at hand, Mr Mandela has a spring in his step and a face full of smiles these days. It is undeniable he has brought his considerable moral authority to bear on the cauldron of politics in the Middle east and already cracks are beginning to appear in the decades-long impasse between Arab and Jew.

This week, positive signs of an imminent peace deal between Israel and Syria became evident after more than four years of silent hostility. Given its powerful position in Arab politics, its proximity to Israel and its mentorship of Lebanon, Syria is seen as a key element in any bid to bring lasting peace to the region. It is not insignificant that Mr Mandela has recently been to Damascus, followed by the large delegation led by Mr Pahad.

In the meantime, Mr Mandela presses ahead with this attempt at solving one of the world's great vexing questions: how to reconcile Arab and Jew. He needs to hurry, though, because in April next year he is expected in Burundi to help bring his magic touch to the vastly troubled Great Lakes region.

For now, the house in Qunu will have to wait, the grandchildren will have to hang on for just a year or two longer and the cattle will grow fat unseen.

46 BUTHELEZI'S BIG YAWN

February 7 2000

There may have been television cameras, photographers and a hundred journalists from around the world arrayed before him, but at 9.25am yesterday morning, Home Affairs Minister Mangouthu Buthelezi couldn't help himself for a moment longer. He yawned.

After almost half an hour of gruff, indecipherable droning by the Minister of Safety and Security Steve Tshwete, who was simply reading from a prepared statement, nobody blamed Dr Buthelezi for his entirely appropriate and natural response.

In fact, not many people saw the yawn, hidden as it was behind a huge emerald ring glinting on the finger of the Minister of Home Affairs. It was probably just as well the gesture remained largely unseen or a sudden epidemic would have cut through the audience, and the assembled ministers, like a veld fire.

The tragedy was that the yawn was exactly what everybody in the room was feeling, including the four other cabinet ministers, who found themselves listening to Mr Tshwete's insufferable presentation of the country's latest anti-crime plan.

In previous years, cabinet ministers used to appear individually before the media to brief them on their plans for the year ahead. Facts and figures were usually bandied about wildly and a whole list of goals and priorities were set.

Of course, these seldom amounted to much but were touted in any case, when delivered by the Safety and Security Minister, as being the government's newest, boldest anti-crime plan blueprint.

Now, however, all the ministers have been grouped together into "clusters" in a symbolic and perhaps even meaningful attempt to improve communication and coordination. This has been one of President Mbeki's innovations and it is impossible to tell at this stage whether it's making any difference at an administrative level.

As regards transparency, it is far tougher to get meaningful responses from six ministers in an hour than it is from one minister in the same time period.

This is particularly the case if one one particular topic, such as spying on the German Embassy, dominates the discussion.

What has been surprising about Briefing Week 2000 so far has been that ministers seem no longer to be prepared to announce a range of hopelessly ambitious plans, accept the glory of the limelight and then disappear into the shadows until next year's briefing. Rather like President Thabo Mbeki on Friday last week, they'd rather say nothing.

The six ministers who occupy the cutting edge of the nation's anti-crime effort limited themselves to a handful of incredibly modest objectives.

The "cluster" had realised after a number of visits to areas of high crime, said Mr Tshwete, that "unless we urgently and seriously tackle to issue of endemic poverty, the fight against crime would not be won".

This, of course, is no news to anybody but it is pleasing that the Cabinet has at least caught up. The cluster said an urban renewal programme would be put in place to deal especially with problems in high-density poverty-ridden areas. This is a good, long-term project but it will make little difference any time soon.

Then the cluster agreed that improved methods of gathering intelligence were necessary (true), that border posts should be upgraded (yes) and that the court process - including delays in the finalisation of cases, reducing the number of awaiting trial prisoners and reducing backlogs - needed to be sped up (about time).

The ministers said human resources needed to be developed and that quality service delivery was a priority (obvious).

The latter referred to upgrading courts, better victim support and quicker computerisation. The ministers added that private sector partnerships were important.

After an hour and a half, mostly confined to embarrassing (Minister of Intelligence) Mr Nhlanhla about the ineptitude of South Africa's "intelligence" service, one was left feeling saddened by the lack of direction or purpose.

Maybe, however, it is more realistic to concentrate on speeding up process and making things more efficient than it is announcing grandiose plans every year which convince nobody and achieve nothing. It's not as exciting but it probably works better, even if it does prompt the odd yawn.

47 DANIE SCHUTTE: STRAIGHT FROM THE FARM

March 24 2000

Parliament's Old Assembly chamber, with its green leather-covered benches, old wood panels and dangling microphones, is a familiar place for Danie Schutte.

For many years he sat here, at the very vortex of National Party power, a trusted, young, pedantic, sharp-tongued politician with a furrowed brow and the arrogant mien of a prosecutor on the hunt. His tenacity is legend.

It was largely due to Mr Schutte's titanic obstructionism that the law establishing the Truth and Reconciliation Commission was amended in 300 places, reproduced in countless drafts, and finally concluded after many months of heated wrangling.

Nothing was allowed to slip by him. He fought for the cause of the National Party like a re-born acolyte, a hyena with the last bone fragment, and his reward was a seat on the government front bench in Parliament, the leadership of the National Party in KwaZulu-Natal, a position on the Transitional Executive Committee (which temporarily governed South Africa until the 1994 election) and a key role at the World Trade Centre negotiations.

But the years have passed and Mr Schutte, still only 52, is a dairy farmer now in the rolling hills of KwaZulu-Natal.

It is obvious that he is not quite ready to return to the land, nor to troublesome tractors, just yet.

"There is life after politics," he told the joint committee on intelligence this week, "but not in agriculture".

Mr Schutte was one of three applicants for the position of Inspector General of the Intelligence Services, all of whom appeared in the Old Assembly chamber on Wednesday.

The post is one of considerable power, allowing unparalleled access to the intelligence-gathering work, secret files and information processing capabilities of the state. Not even the president will have such untrammelled clearance.

On top of that, the intelligence service is in a bit of a mess at the moment after a chronology of embarrassingly inept operations carried out with all the dignity of the Keystone Cops.

As a result, there are some sensitivities over who should be put in the Inspector General's chair.

On paper, Mr Schutte is well qualified for the position. He has served as the deputy minister for intelligence, was a member not long ago of the very committee now interrogating him and wrote most of the legislation which created the position for which he was now applying. His legal background (he was State Advocate), commercial, political, and governmental knowledge are all weighty. The highlights of his career, as he told the committee, was nothing other than "being involved in creating the new South Africa".

But, frankly, he hasn't a snowball's chance in hell of getting the nod.

The fact that he realised this made his appearance slightly pathetic, his grilling a little cruel, and the prospect of his return to the milking shed a touch tragic.

When asked at the end if he had anything to add, Mr Schutte replied: "You've given me such a rough time, I'm tempted to keep you all here for another hour". This was not the response of a man who expects to move back to

Pretoria next month.

The ANC were quite entitled to dig up all they could to scuttle Mr Schutte's chances. He had been their adversary often enough and they distrust both his past and his motives enough to justify a little extra effort.

One ANC MP, Mahlangu Mninwa, went so far as to quote from a motion proposed by a certain Mr DPA Schutte on Friday 5 March 1982 in which the aforesaid urged the government not to bother training local people because "it takes a very, very long time and frequently has limited results".

The beauty of the question was that it was used to cast a shadow on Mr Schutte's sincerity when he responded earlier that "train, train, train" was his plan for the intelligence services.

This was no casual quote found accidentally amongst old papers. This was one arrow from the quiver of revenge.

Indeed, casting doubt was about the committee could do for Mr Schutte, after 22 years in Parliament, is too slippery, too experienced to fall into anything quite so obvious as a trick question. Instead, through their line or questioning, MPs implied he may yet be fingered by the Truth and Reconciliation Commission for human rights abuses, he must have been involved in some dirty business when previously deputy minister of intelligence and he can't possibly have given up party politics.

As if to prove the last point, Mr Schutte blanched at the overly sympathetic attentions of the National Party's Martha Olckers (who also nominated him for the post). "I don't need to be protected," he told Ms Olckers through gritted teeth.

Denials made little difference, however, particularly with a dash every now and then of that old arrogant attitude and the odd inappropriate, betraying remark.

"There were some human rights abuses by the ANC but that doesn't tar every member of the ANC," Mr Schutte pointed out with a straight face. Then later,

"If you have a problem in Venda, do you think a white man from the Cape will really be able to assess what's happening there?"

But these are idiosyncrasies of a different era, as vanished in Parliament as the stain by Verwoerd's old seat.

As if to make sure things went the ANC's way, the party's Chief Whip, Tony Yengeni, arrived for a while to watch proceedings. He wore a t-shirt with the logo "the logical choice" inscribed on the back. We can safely assume he was not referring to the man who is now back tending his cows and his memories in the early Autumn mornings.

48 NJABULO NDEBELE: 'THERE ARE MANY KINDS OF AFRICAN IDENTITY'

April 13 2000

You will find Njabulo Ndebele at the end of an oak-lined avenue in a Cape Dutch house once occupied by Cecil John Rhodes.

It is a house filled with the material relics of a colonial past: green window shutters and white stone walls, brass latches and Oregon doors, sun-drenched patios, and thick, grey vines.

It is a past that is different from but not alien to Ndebele's own. For the new vice-chancellor of the University of Cape Town has never been one to shirk new experiences, from wherever they come, nor to deny their validity for a fuller understanding of a South African life and identity.

"I weave in and out of cultural contexts," he says, "and I like it that way. I've grown to put a high price on that.

"I find myself sitting in Cecil John Rhodes's house and it's just part of this journey of discovery."

It is a journey that has taken the 52-year-old from the streets of Western Native Township in the 1940s to exile in Lesotho in the 1970s, from the stone halls of Cambridge to the Rocky Mountains of Colorado, from the University of the

North to Rhodes's house on the slopes of Table Mountain. With every step, Ndebele has been questioning, wondering, writing, and picking apart the stereotypes and assumptions he detests with such passion.

He is the archetypal intellectual. He thinks not only deeply but laterally. His language is littered with considered notions.

"The absence of violence doesn't necessarily mean the presence of peace," he throws out in mid-discussion.

His ideas, though, are not couched in academic pretensions.

They are just as likely to be illustrated by a traditional African fable.

The ease with which he slips into theoretical constructs of life, society, race, and the universe reminds one of Thabo Mbeki.

Indeed, in his new post at the head of what is arguably South Africa's foremost academic institution, his attitudes will carry growing import in the Mbeki era.

The notions both of an African identity as well as of an African renaissance are appealing to mull over and dissect. Their attraction is that they define collectively not only whom we think we are but where would like to be going.

"There are many kinds of African identity," he argues. "And no one single essentialist definition. We may have to wait a hundred years before we begin to see what characterises a South African identity.

Identity, in other words, whether personal, national, or continental, derives from experience. The broader and more varied the experience, the more defined and distinctive the identity.

This is partly why Ndebele is so comfortable from a personal point of viewpoint, assimilating day to day life in New York's Greenwich Village with policy formulation in one of the country's best-known universities.

The African renaissance, too, needs to be freed from a number of increasingly common assumptions, he argues.

"I am an old enemy of slogans and unearned labels," he wrote in an article on Eurocentrism published in *The Sunday Independent* in 1997.

"The African renaissance is not an ideology," he says now, leaning forward on a gleaming antique table. "It is not a series of rules by which this continent can be made into a success. It is the ability to recognise positive trends and to push them forward.

"What it means for the government, as well as for universities, is to be constantly scanning the horizon for these things."

Signs of renaissance can be found everywhere. In Duduza, for instance, where Ndebele's family still live, the unlikely heralds of the renaissance are dented, old Mazda 323s. The cars, as Ndebele discovered on his return from New York (where he was a prestigious Ford Foundation writer-in-residence), pick up the local people and take them anywhere they want to go in the township for R2.

At first, the traditional minibus taxi organisations objected to the new phenomenon, but the community made it clear this was what they wanted.

The development has unlocked immense possibilities, says Ndebele. It means the more efficient movement of people, a fledgling spare parts industry and further evidence of the constant willingness of many communities around the country to improve themselves and their conditions of life.

Ndebele spent several tough years in the 1990s as the rector of the University of the North (Turfloop). The experience was a humbling one that tested his own qualities of perseverance and resilience to the limit.

"Any situation people find themselves in will either make them stronger or beat them," he says.

Confronted by the enormous obstacles facing the "historically black universities" it would have been easy to have been depressed and achieve nothing.

Ndebele was realistic enough to acknowledge that while he did what he could, the challenge of turning the fortunes of institutions like Turfloop around was the work of a lifetime and possibly of several generations.

"I had to be humble about what I could achieve."

Taking up the reins at UCT has thrust Ndebele into the mainstream of black intellectual life. But that, too, has its challenges.

He warns openly of the dangers of centralising military, economic and political power in the hands of a small ruling clique. He also empathises with the ideas of his predecessor, Mamphela Ramphele, that refraining from a critique of the new government, in spite of its role in the overthrow of apartheid, means trouble.

"I liked what Ramphele said about avoiding a culture of silence immediately. But I don't believe there is silence already or that decay has settled in. Citizens of a democracy have to be vigilant. They have a responsibility not to give up certain rights and obligations out of good intention.

"Democracy means people participating with knowledge. If they don't have the ability to synthesise these ideas, they are disempowered. It is the responsibility of all to ensure people are aware of their responsibilities and are aware of the danger of allowing an easy consensus to abrogate their responsibilities."

Ndebele has strong views on national reconciliation. One of his deepest regrets is missing out on the human rights violations hearings in Duduza, his hometown where, incidentally, the first incident of necklacing took place.

"The moral basis of South Africa's capitalism is heavily flawed. Its rampant accumulation is spilling over into day-to-day personal relations and now we are reaping the fruits.

"Black victims have begun to participate because they think they can get away with it. The solution to moral decay: 'we have to be hard-nosed'."

That means more resources for the police as well as the improvement and wide application of effective administrative systems.

"The biggest challenge is to put in place a process which will allow us to identify when the system is being abused."

Also important for moral regeneration is the re-thinking of the way South African children are being taught: "We need to look at the way we teach our history, the way we teach our poetry, the way we teach our novels, the way we revamp our museums, the way we reflect on the way we think."

Part of apartheid's power, Ndebele contends, was its ability to reinforce stereotypes and simplify perceptions. The challenge both to democracy and to the intellectual is to rejoin what apartheid tore apart.

"We have to engage apartheid on our own terms". That means looking out for the positive. It means breaking down stereotypes and exploding myths, humanising marginalised communities and wrestling with the idea of what it means to be a South African, and an African, at this point in our history.

That is Ndebele's message. Rhodes would undoubtedly have found him a worthy adversary.

49 THABO MBEKI, THE SUPERPOWER AND THE DALAI LAMA

November 28 2000

President Thabo Mbeki's refusal to meet Tibetan spiritual leader Dalai Lama on a one-to-one personal basis encapsulates much of what it is to be a small, developing country in the world at the turn of the 20th century.

It is a world in which pragmatism often takes precedence over principle and in which the moral high ground is shrouded in the mist of expedience.

Ever since former president Nelson Mandela cast off the country's ties so dramatically and impetuously with Taiwan in early 1997, it has been obvious that South Africa has thrown its lot in with the People's Republic of China.

The recent visit of former Chinese premier and current chairman of the the PRC's legislature, Li Peng, to South Africa and the simultaneous trip of a large delegation of members of the ANC's national executive committee together with provincial secretaries to Beijing for a strategic planning session, is a clear reminder that our wagon is hitched to a red star.

The benefits from such a relationship could well be profound.

Few doubt that in the next century, China will achieve the status of the world's great superpower. The sheer numbers of people, their work ethic, their implicit regard for the value of education and their access to vast resources dictate that this must be so.

It is a process that has already received a fillip by the incorporation of the economic dynamo of Hong Kong and is likely to be given further momentum following America's recent agreement with China over its joining of the World Trade Organisation (WTO).

Though there is still some way to go before the eastern giant's membership of the WTO has been ratified, the inevitable will soon see the rapid opening of China's massive, 1.2-billion person market to global trade.

There can hardly be a more significant moment in world history than this. It is Hannibal harnessing the elephant, the discovery of gunpowder, the splitting of the atom. The question is: can Africa afford to be left behind once more?

We all know that Beijing has an extremely poor record of human rights abuse. Tibet is just one of several hotspots of oppression, ranging from religious cults and the democracy movement to secessionists within the country.

As far as South Africa is concerned, it is the old issue of whether more can be achieved from within or in conflict with the body that requires transformation. The analogy of urinating into a tent, or out from it, occurs.

The ANC, and particularly President Mbeki, learned during the years of struggle that outside pressure, while helpful, was seldom the means for fundamental change. South Africa's own democratic revolution was acquired not by trade embargoes not by border skirmishes but by the actions of the people and by negotiations and compromise among the leaders.

Information, the circulation of ideas, knowledge, communication: these are the AK47s of the modern revolution. This, too, will be true of China.

In the same way that change is inevitable in China, so it requires delicate management.

The collapse of the world's most populous nation into civil war would be a global catastrophe. By the same token, its embracing of democracy and free trade would be a triumph.

President Mbeki has announced a clear and unambiguous agenda in his dealings on the world stage. That is, the eradication of poverty.

He emphasised this earlier in the month at the Commonwealth Heads of Government Meeting in Durban, has said it repeatedly at home since his election to the highest office and he will say it again in Seattle at the World Trade Organisation summit.

In a sense, the Mandela-era plan that South Africa should represent the moral high ground as the warrior for global human rights, has been downgraded. It remains important, and wherever possible will be pursued, but it is not the lodestone of our foreign policy anymore. Now, we are the champions of the poor.

Human rights and the eradication of poverty are not mutually exclusive objectives. They are intimately inter-linked. We just have more room to manoeuvre under the poverty banner and the cause is more pan-African and in keeping with Third World solidarity than the celebration and trumpeting of our own individual achievement.

President Mbeki's decision to meet the Dalai Lama only as part of a larger delegation of others here to celebrate the parliament of world religions, is an uncomfortable situation which highlights the complexities and contradictions of politics in the world today.

It feels like we are being bullied into denying our hard-fought principles and stirs concerns that a world led by the PRC will be a worse place for it.

President Mbeki's task, along with other world leaders, will be to ensure that this is not the case and that the Chinese century will be a halcyon one for democracy, for the poor and for Africa.

50 NKOSAZANA ZUMA: 'AFRICA NEEDS TO FIND ITS OWN SOLUTIONS'

February 8 2000

Do you know, asks a minister who does know, what happened to foreign minister Nkosazana Zuma recently in the Democratic Republic of Congo?

"She went so deep into the bush to assist with the peace talks that she almost got caught up in the fighting". They had to pull her out at the last minute, chortles the minister, but she didn't want to go.

This week, as she addressed the media and assorted diplomats in Parliament, it was obvious that Dr Zuma is rather enjoying her work on the international stage as democratic South Africa's second foreign minister.

At a time when Africa itself is becoming more expressive about its needs and more demanding about its place in the world, the continent could hardly have a better champion more accustomed to awkward situations.

She is as doughty, impervious and stubborn as when she headed the health ministry, but she also seems more confident, her voice a little less wavery. Her sober comments are spiced with jokes and stories, but the unavoidable point is never long in the making.

Like, for instance, when she spoke of the United Nations and the need for it to get involved in peacekeeping and problem-solving in Africa but also of the need, perhaps even more important, for Africa to find its own solutions.

To illustrate the point she told a parable: There's a beautiful, hard, strong stick in the next village. It's a very good stick. But it's of no use if the snake is here, in this village.

In other words, she explained, we can look to the UN for support but we need to find the solution here using Africa's "own strength, our own experience, our own history".

Zuma spoke at length on a whole range of issues from Angola and Namibia to fascism in Europe. At times, she knows the stance she is adopting is controversial.

South Africa's attitude to Angola, for instance, that there can be no military solution, is apparently far from the consensus position even among African countries. But Dr Zuma is right in saying that Unita will probably never be defeated by virtue of its guerrilla-style flexibility and that even if Unita miraculously beat the MPLA-government, the world would not accept its credentials.

At other times, Zuma is adept at avoiding the question as she ever was when the Democratic Party's Mike Elllis was on his feet demanding answers in the national assembly.

Asked whether South Africa believed China had a democratically elected government and whether we were ignoring its human rights record, Dr Zuma replied: "China has a government. We recognise it, work with it and will continue working with it."

A classic piece of denial, politician-style.

But Zuma is a different creature now from the one which stalked the front benches under the Mandela administration. Now, as she criss-crosses the world full of grand notions of renaissance, peace, and multilateral co-operation, she can afford to marvel at the antics of her colleagues in the chamber.

As if to illustrate this idea, Dr Zuma related another story.

A diplomat colleague was visiting Africa, she told the briefing, and one day called home to check on his 5-year-old son. The child said, "Dad, have you seen any lions yet?" The diplomat said "No, not yet son". The child said, "Dad, have you seen any tigers yet?" The diplomat said "No, not yet son". The child said, "Dad, have you seen any elephants yet?" The diplomat said "No, not yet son". The child said, "well, what have you seen?"

"I've seen a lot of politicians," replied the diplomat.

"Oh," said the child. "What kind of animal is that?"

Looking at yesterday's line-up of ministers, in which Dr Zuma has blossomed into a new person and Environmental Affairs and Tourism minister Valli Moosa has thrown off his pinstripe suits in favour of t-shirts and chinos, a politician is an animal which has the capacity to change its spots.

51 ALEC ERWIN: 'I'VE NEVER BEEN A UTOPIAN COMMUNIST'

Wednesday 9 February 2000

Just because Trade and Industry minister Alec Erwin and Public Enterprises minister Jeff Radebe serve on the central committee of the South African Communist Party, doesn't mean they can't be as committed to free enterprise as the next person.

Communism, you see, has moved on from centralised economies, five-year plans, state interventionism and bigger bureaucracies. That all went 20 years ago with Perestroika and the Iron Curtain.

Now anybody can be a communist, as long as the fundamental objective is securing the interests of "ordinary people" in the long-term.

The end, in other words, justifies the means.

According to Mr Erwin, who addressed a ministerial briefing in Parliament yesterday: "I've never been a utopian socialist and I never joined a utopian communist party".

Reality is the clarion call for the modern communist in the new millennium, even in South Africa.

Indeed, Radebe, far from being reluctant to show enthusiasm about his current portfolio - which is essentially the chopping up and selling of state assets together with a bit of job slashing on the side - actually managed to argue he was at the forefront of the communist vanguard. And with a straight face too.

"Even my work is not a contradiction," he said with ringing, even plausible conviction.

Mr Erwin barely flinched when asked yesterday whether it was forbidden to say the "p" word (privatisation) in government circles. He said it immediately ("if it's being sold off, it's privatisation"), and so did Radebe, repeatedly. Perhaps they had been practising together before the briefing.

Communism is so broad and pragmatic these days that privatisation and job cuts are perfectly reasonable components of communist policy. Indeed, they are essential to the macro-economic planning of any serious Marxist because they are in the eventual interest of the masses.

"There has been no ideological conversion to the free market," said Mr Erwin of both his own and the ANC's obvious non-conversion. "There has never been such a thing in the history of the world". A free market, in other words, is just like a free lunch.

For Mr Radebe, neither was there any discomfort at all in reconciling "inevitable job losses" with his place at the helm of the proletarian vanguard.

As clumsy as it all was, the two ministers made two points that deserve a restating.

First, privatisation is one end of a scale of things which might happen to a parastatal or state asset. To call all joint ventures, strategic partner appointments, commercialisations and partial sell-offs the same thing, privatisation, is misleading. It is also cruel and unusual punishment to keep making communists say the word and, as such, is against the Constitution.

Second, the failure to reform and restructure "the state" in its broadest form, from camping sites to nuclear power facilities, and instead take on onerous levels of national debt would be, in the words of Erwin, both "suicidal and stupid".

As for communism? Well, it's really entirely up to you. One size fits all.

52 NGCONDE BALFOUR: A MINISTERIAL OUTSWINGER

Thursday 10 February 2000

You don't ever really want to get on the wrong side of Ngconde Balfour, the minister of sport and recreation.

He has a certain intimidating presence that can only partially be explained by his prop forward-like physique.

It is something more than that: a smile you're not sure is genuine, eyes a little smaller and a little more searching that you would like, a pleasant demeanour you suspect is fragile.

Like his slow-medium bowling action, which has caught many a press gallery batsman off-guard, he hides a venomous, nasty outswing in his languid delivery.

It is wise to stay alert.

Why else would virtually every sporting federation in the country fall over themselves to sign one year transformation performance agreements if they didn't think Mr Balfour was capable of wielding the stick.

As he told the assembled journalists and diplomats at a parliamentary briefing yesterday: "I don't expect excuses when assessment time comes round". There will be some very worried sports administrators in a few months from now.

You would immediately be getting off on the wrong foot if you addressed Mr Balfour merely as the minister of sport. He doesn't like that. He will interrupt huffily with the words " .... and recreation", referring to the other part of his ministerial responsibilities, and you will remember not to do it again.

Perhaps what gives the minister of sport and recreation his edge is what he himself describes as his fanaticism. While he obviously enjoys a little recreation, he simply loves sport.

He kicked off his briefing yesterday with a bit of a confession.

"I am nervous," he said, speaking in anticipation of last night's big soccer game between South Africa and Nigeria.

"Most people won't be able to breathe between 5.30 and 7.30. Me, I'm going to sit by myself and I don't want anyone to phone or disturb me. I know one thing, I am passionate about South African sport. I suppose I am a fanatic."

It is probably true to say that if every cabinet minister was as fanatical about their portfolio as Mr Balfour is of his, President Mbeki's delivery problem would be not nearly as worrying.

"There is no denying that vestiges of racism in sport still remain as a legacy of our past," Mr Balfour intoned weightily. "There is a perception that among coaches, selectors and even players there is a reluctance to embrace transformation in sport and this is manifested in their approach to especially team selections". Then the coup de grace: "Such blatant racism by a small group will be eradicated as there is absolutely no place for such individuals in sport."

I think we are clear on that now. Strangely, though, as he was nearing the end of his speech, Mr Balfour trailed off. "Why am I reading this as if I'm a stuck cassette" he asked, rhetorically of course.

Perhaps his heart and mind were far off on a dusty field in Lagos where the hopes of a nation were resting, indirectly, on his broad shoulders.

53 WESTERN CAPE POLITICS: THE AGONY AND THE ECSTASY

February 16 2000

There was a clearly discernible smile on the face of Western Cape Premier Gerald Morkel yesterday afternoon as he bowed slowly and formally to the ANC leader of the opposition, Ebrahim Rasool.

The bow always takes place when a provincial parliament begins a sitting. This time, though, the bows were a little more extravagant, the smile a little less well hidden, than would usually have been the case.

Mr Morkel's bow said 'take your no confidence motion and shove it, Ebrahim' and Mr Rasool's said 'I'll get you next time, Gerald'. But no words were spoken.

If things had been different, if the ANC had succeeded in its bid to break up the coalition government this week, Mr Morkel's speech yesterday afternoon could very well have been his last as premier.

He may even have been asked, on his way out of the chamber, for the keys to his glorious house Leeuwenhof.

Instead, Mr Morkel glowed with the confidence of a victor, stood with the arrogant gait of a matador and could hardly wait to begin to rub salt in the wounds of the ANC benches opposite.

At the far end of the New NP bench, like a naughty schoolboy told to sit in the corner, was Peter Marais, the villain of the day.

Sitting silent and sullen as a statue, the sacked minister barely moved for the hour it took Mr Morkel to work his way through his speech. With arms crossed and an expression as gloomy as the skies over Mpumalanga, he probably sat there wishing the earth would swallow him up.

At one end of the New NP bench sat agony, at the other, ecstasy rose to address the public.

"You and your cohorts are nothing more than political delinquents," said Mr Morkel, warming to his task, relishing the gathering chorus of heckles and shouts. The desk microphones on the ANC benches flickered like Christmas lights as they picked up short interjections cast in anger across the floor.

"You sold your soul for Leeuwenhof," shouted the ANC's Cameron Dugmore. His microphone flashed briefly. Mr Dugmore heckled and twittered throughout Mr Morkel's speech like a cicada at sunset. But nobody really minded because everyone in the chamber had read how Mr Dugmore was forced to put off his honeymoon in Mauritius to help overthrow the New NP.

"It's called discipline," said mr Dugmore to jeers from across the blue carpet.

Mr Morkel actually began to taunt the ANC. "It is obvious the ANC will never reconcile themselves with the fact that they are not part of this cabinet," he ranted. "This is not a circus, the clowns are in the audience," he railed.

All the while, Mr Rasool sat hunched and mostly impassive, his right knee shaking up and down with nervous energy, his left hand endlessly fiddling with a pen. Occasionally he would chide Mr Morkel with a barbed remark.

Hennie Bester, meanwhile, the Democratic Party's kingmaker, sat paying scant attention to the jousting between Mr Rasool and Mr Morkel. His bearing spoke of a grim satisfaction. So heedless was he of the political theatre being played out before him, and so confident of its outcome, that Mr Bester concentrated on two more important things. Indeed, he wrote so much and so quickly, page after page, that one would have thought he was in an exam and had only ten minutes to finish the essay.

It was only at the end of the proceedings, after Mr Morkel had finished his speech and Mr Rasool was explaining why the ANC had decided to withdraw the no confidence motion, that Mr Bester interrupted proceedings with a scrupulously correct point of order. "He's making a political speech," insisted Mr Bester, with an expression of amusement on his face.

"You are absolutely correct," conceded the Speaker. "He is dragging it out a bit long".

And so the ANC's bid to rule the Cape came to an end. Mr Morkel went home to Leeuwenhof. Mr Marais went off to wait for the disciplinary hearing he now faces. Mr Cameron would probably try to catch the next flight to Mauritius and Mr Rasool would return to the drawing board to plan, once more, how to win the premiership that seemed, just for three days, so close to his grasp.

54 PATRICK MCKENZIE: ET TU, BRUTÉ?

February 18 2000

Treachery has a time-honoured place in the noble art of politics.

For millennia, great people - and not a small number of ordinary ones - have been betrayed, cheated, duped and stabbed in the back, metaphorically and on occasion literally by those they considered their close friends and most reliable allies.

Shakespeare calls such treachery "the most unkindest cut of all" in what is perhaps the definitive tale of grand deceit and disloyalty, Julius Caesar.

It was no coincidence, then, that the most famous words from that great tragedy, "et tu, Bruté?" were uttered in no more august a chamber than the Western Cape provincial parliament this week by none other than the premier, Gerald Morkel.

For treachery and deceit were very much on the mind of the premier this week.

But rather than sacked cabinet minister Peter Marais being the object of the premier's derision, in fact it was a certain Patrick McKenzie, Member of the Provincial Legislature, formerly of the new National Party and now sitting on the front bench of the African National Congress who bore the brunt of the premier's attention on the subject of treachery.

"You may have been able to buy Patrick McKenzie," Mr Morkel railed at the ANC benches on Wednesday afternoon. "But do you really need more egg on your face?"

"Ask Allan Hendrickse about Brutus," he instructed ANC leader Ebrahim

Rasool, "who sat as close to him as he is sitting next to you now before he knifed him in the back".

It was dramatic stuff, what did it mean?

Some years ago, back in the days of PW Botha's Tricameral Parliament, Mr McKenzie promised Mr Hendrickse his unfailing support in the face of a number of threatened defections from the Labour Party to the National Party.

When the trickle of defections became a flood and the flood became the majority of Labour Party members, Mr McKenzie jumped ship. Mr Morkel, who was also a Labour Party stalwart at the time, has never forgotten the betrayal.

"Patrick promises and lied then, Patrick promises and lies now," Mr Morkel warned, before culminating in that classic line of treachery unveiled: "et tu, bruté?"

But seeing as Mr Morkel chose Julius Caesar to illustrate his feelings toward certain members of the Western Cape Legislature, let us continue with the analogy, just for fun.

There are a number of lines from the great play that have a certain entirely coincidental familiarity to current events and characters.

Take this, for instance: "Seldom he smiles, and smiles in such a sort; As if he mocked himself and scorned his spirit; That could be moved to smile at anything."

That has to be Mr Marais, sitting stony-faced and inscrutable at the far end of the New NP bench. With his cabinet privileges at risk and a disciplinary hearing pending, little wonder indeed that he didn't smile once during the premier's speech on Wednesday afternoon.

What about: "It is the bright day that brings forth the adder. And that craves wary walking". That surely must be a reference to the ANCs launching of a no confidence motion at just the time the New NP had managed to purge itself of the unhappy Mr Marais. Thus, the deadly snake emerges in the sunlight.

What better words for the new DP-New NP coalition than the call: “Never come such division ‘tween our souls!”

But a word of warning, too, that in politics, self-interest will always outweigh loyalty to a larger body and that those one trusts may be up to more than you might think. Hence, the Bard may have cast the DP’s Hennie Bester as the dangerous Cassius: “Yond Cassius has a lean and hungry look, He thinks too much: such men are dangerous”.

Certainly, there was a sense on Wednesday, as Mr Morkel replied to the debate on his opening of parliament speech, that important matters were afoot, that governments could change and opportunities could present themselves. But there was also an understanding that the ANC could move too early, expose the dissenters within the New NP before time and use up the one annual no confidence motion without success.

“There is a tide in the affairs of men,” remarks Caesar about the difficulties of judging exactly the right moment to act, “Which, taken at the flood, leads on to fortune: Omitted, all the voyage of their life, Is bound in shallows and miseries.”

But while Mr Morkel may have enjoyed casting himself in the part of Caesar the emperor, there are two sobering points to be made.

First, for all his noblesse, Caesar did get knifed in the back by his buddies and, as a result, was removed rather forcefully from office.

Second, the Ides of March named as Caesar’s doomsday by the soothsayer is actually the Fifteenth of March. That gives Morkel just under a month.

55 THE THREE WISE MEN OF EUROPE

Thursday 16 March 2000

Three European ambassadors graced the committee rooms of the national parliament this week bringing a touch of eloquence, considerable learning and not a little grace under fire to bear on the discussion of the awkward topic of trade.

The specific subject was, of course, the protracted negotiations surrounding a Free Trade Agreement recently implemented on a provisional basis between the European Union and South Africa and the occasion was the enlightenment of the portfolio committee on foreign affairs.

Anybody paying attention to the arduous negotiations, which have gone on for at least four years, will have noticed the whole thing has become a bit mucky of late over the issue of various wine and spirit labels such as sherry and port.

In the words of EU ambassador Michael Laidler, "we were grappling with grappa and trying to discover whose ouzo was whose".

At first the three ambassadors, being the delightfully expressive Mr Laidler, the tall, hulking but noble frame of French ambassador Tristan D'Albi and the slim, mustachioed Portuguese ambassador, Manuel Pereira, were in a comfortable even happy mood.

Mr Pereira, who spoke first according to protocol as he represents the country holding the presidency of the EU, even depicted the diplomats as "the three musketeers". So good natured were they one expected them to leap up at any moment, cross their pens and should "All for one and one for all!"

They believed, so they said, that the free trade agreement was jolly good for their own countries and was jolly good for South Africa too. It was "visionary", enthused Mr Laidler, "extremely important," agreed Mr Pereira, "really good for South Africa" confirmed Mr D'Albi.

The ambassadors also heartily congratulated South Africa for our famous march to democracy ("we admire you", said Mr Pereira) and pounded us on the back for being so co-operative in boosting North-South relations ("very forward-looking").

Imagine the surprise of the three musketeers when not only were they not acclaimed as old friends and served more cheese scones with their tea, but they were rudely rounded upon by the representatives of the South African masses.

The first to stick in the sabre was Pallo Jordan, the sacked minister of environmental affairs and tourism who is getting his kicks out of committee room muggings.

Nobody has ever doubted Mr Jordan's intelligence. Some even argue this has been the most dangerous stumbling block to his political career.

The EU, Mr Jordan contended, had conducted its bargaining with South Africa in the spirit - to use the words of Adam Smith - of "petty monopoly". The ambassadors looked stung. "When it comes to your own economies, you want to exercise protection," Mr Jordan insisted.

Next to pile in was Mewa Ramgobin, an ANC MP from KwaZulu-Natal. Everyone knew that South Africa and Europe enjoyed long and deep historical ties, Mr Ramgobin argued. But did this not mean there was a historical responsibility toward Africa by its former colonisers to negotiate trade agreements in good faith?

The ambassadors were unsettled. They gesticulated their hands as if they were duelling amongst themselves. They called over aides. But they never, not for a moment, lost their cool.

Even when Mr D'Albi said, "I feel personally attacked", he said it with a smile, as if someone had asked him to speak but had got the language confused and instead told him his country was going to the dogs.

The unflappable Mr Laidler used a slightly different approach. He agreed with Mr Jordan.

"I believe he is, to a degree, correct," Mr Laidler ventured, adding both South African and EU negotiators were "adults" and that "if negotiations are to be meaningful, there has to be something in it for everybody".

It is not as if we got sneaky at the last minute and put new demands on the table like Houdini pulling something out of a hat, he said.

In almost the same breath, Mr Laidler reached over and tapped a thick document sitting in front of him. It was just like, well, pulling something out of a hat.

Here is an analysis of the agreement which clearly shows that this is one of the least protectionist trade agreements that exist, Mr Laidler said.

Frankly, the three ambassadors were becoming a little irritated.

"When I started in the foreign office 33 years ago," said Mr D'Albi, "I was involved in trade negotiations with the Spanish over wine. Trade agreements take three years on average to conclude, sometimes up to 5 years and still they can fail and leave blood on the windows".

"I certainly don't want to respond in a way that could be seen as provocative," Mr Laidler declared in response to a pointed question from ANC MP Ben Turok.

But with all the "hurly-burly" over protectionism, Mr Laidler thought it pertinent to remind the rabble before him just who these three people were who were sitting before them taking it on the chin.

The EU gives South Africa R800-million a year in development aid and its constituent 15 members are responsible for more than three quarters of all aid inflows. Trade between the EU and South Africa accounts for 40 percent of South Africa's total trade amounting to some R16-billion per annum. Seventy percent of direct foreign investment in South Africa comes from the EU and 90 percent of all South Africa's foreign investment is placed in EU countries.

It was a polite reminder, in the most diplomatic way, of whose foot the shoe is really on and whose ouzo is really whose.

When it's all for one and one for all, the three musketeers always win.

56 GEORGE FIVAZ: 'THE COLLAPSE OF VALUES MAKES POLICING DIFFICULT'

March 24 2000

National Police commissioner George Fivaz will never forget the day in his boyhood when he sat at home one lunchtime with his family and listened to the wireless (radio).

On it, news of the Rivonia Trial crackled through to listeners in the dusty Free State town of Bultfontein. The wireless announced that Nelson Mandela and the other Rivonia trialists had been sentenced to life imprisonment for sabotage and high treason. The family were delighted. Mandela had got what he deserved.

"Life is strange," Mr Fivaz told me this week. "Never in my wildest dreams did I think that one day the man being sentenced would appoint me his commissioner of police. But life takes its own direction sometimes and its impact can never be known.

"I wasn't clued up about the background at that age and what really inspired those people and what really sparked Mandela and his followers to do what they did."

The name Fivaz is of Swiss extraction, not Portuguese or Greek as he is sometimes asked. His forbears left Switzerland in the 14th century, moved to Britain for a while and then joined the exodus to South Africa in the 1650s.

"When I look at Switzerland now I can't understand why they left. But I suppose Switzerland was a different place in the 1400s. The whole country had been burnt to the ground and it wasn't a pleasant place like now".

Born in Reitz in the Free State in December 1945, Mr Fivaz grew up in Bultfontein, the son of a farmer and businessman.

The family were not what he terms "super-Afrikaners". They mostly supported the United Party and a certain spirit of rebellion flared up amongst his extended kin from time to time. As a child, Mr Fivaz played happily with other children, black and white, without any thought of the racial complexities developing in the land.

"There were racial barriers at school, but we played together and weren't aware of all of that".

Back in those days, in Bultfontein, the police service was considered an honourable profession in which serving the public was the principal objective.

The town was "nothing peculiar, nothing extraordinary", just a pleasant place far from "the real evil" of high crime in the distant cities and isolated from the the nascent anti-apartheid struggle. When Mr Fivaz's elder brother joined the police, he too decided to follow suit.

He started as a student constable helping out at the charge office and, once he had joined properly, was sent off to the Pretoria Police College in 1964. From there it was a succession of assignments across the country from detective branch to narcotics, from one city to another.

Says his official resume: "He is an ordinary policeman and came through the ranks in the normal way".

On two occasions during his career, Mr Fivaz was asked if he would like to join the infamous Security Branch, but each time he declined. "I was never really interested in joining the Security Branch. I wasn't sure what those people were doing behind the curtains and the iron doors. Even later, as a senior policeman,

I didn't know what they were up to. They had their own inspectorate and did their own thing".

As it turned out, the decision not to join the branch was a fortuitous one. It made him more palatable to the new government and saw him become the country's first commissioner of police not to have gone through the Special Branch mill.

Mr Fivaz's political awakening took root at the university of the Orange Free State in the early 1970s. He was studying part-time for a B. Admin degree and took a course in political science.

"Already in those days I realised this process of separate development was never going to work out. If you didn't give communities' capacity or infrastructure, in time the bubble was going to burst. If you didn't give communities a proper and well-defined destination, your plans were not going to work."

At the end of 1976, Mr Fivaz settled in Pretoria and moved in to police management. He joined the National Inspectorate of the South African Police and travelled the world learning about issues like restructuring, decentralisation and strategic planning.

But it was really during the negotiations era in the early 1990s that Mr Fivaz began to make his mark.

He took part, behind the scenes, in drawing up the Groote Schuur and Pretoria Minutes - agreements which ended the armed struggle - and assisted in work on the country's new Constitution.

During this time, he came into frequent contact with the country's future leadership, rubbing shoulders on a daily basis with the ANC's hierarchy including Joe Modise, Thabo Mbeki, Joe Slovo, Nelson Mandela and Joe Nhlanhla.

"I got on with most of them," he says.

He was in appointed in 1993 to an advisory panel on the police set up by

Sydney Mufamadi, who in 1994 became the minister for safety and security. His lack of a clouded Security Branch past, his open-mindedness and his knowledge of strategic planning saw him elevated to Mr Mufamadi's staff full-time from 1994.

He became the obvious choice when Mandela started looking around for someone to head the police force and he was appointed national commissioner on January 29, 1995.

During his research and planning, Mr Fivaz realised there was little the world could teach South Africa about its own unique problems. These included a long history of racial intolerance and even hatred within the police, the amalgamation of 11 police agencies into one and deep-rooted community antipathy to the law and its enforcers. Where existing models were tried out, they inevitably ended in failure.

"We were not privileged in South Africa to have recipes or models for doing what we are doing now. In many cases we relied heavily on experience from outside police sources and in most cases they flopped."

The New York model, or "broken windows" policy for instance, states that you must start with fixing the small things, like broken windows, and the more serious crimes will be easier to control.

"But they don't have political intolerance, taxi wars, gangsters, and Pagad in New York. They didn't know anything about these scenarios. Not many countries can tell us how to handle our racist past and how to remove that from society. They can do that when it comes to our sexist past but no-one could tell us how to remove our racist legacy."

In addition, the poor levels of education among the police - almost a quarter are functionally illiterate - was not something with which many other countries had to contend.

"We had to design our own system and our own process. We had to reinvent the wheel and it wasted a lot of time".

After five years in the hot seat, Mr Fivaz is proud of his role in transforming the police and disappointed with persistently high levels of crime.

"When I'm in black communities, people come up to me and say, 'we're praying for you' and 'we support you'. That never happened in the past. Community support is the most vital part of our job and it's getting better day by day, month by month."

Mr Fivaz is also proud that inter-racial hatred within the police has been controlled and lessened.

"Although we are not where we want to be, we have moved from a position of hate. There is still tension, but not hate in most cases."

Credit for this falls mainly at the feet of the change management team created in 1994. The team met with groups of police officers day and night, hearing their problems and grievances and talking about attitudes.

"I must tell you, it worked," he says. "There are still levels of hate, but it is not destroying relationships totally and in most cases the situation can be defused."

As an indication of how morale is improving in the police, Mr Fivaz says the 30 percent illegal absentee rate of two years ago has fallen to 5 percent. "That in itself tells you a story".

On the downside, (racial) representivity in the police is not where it should be and crime continues to exact a toll on South African communities.

The representivity issue appears to be in hand, with even the senior management echelon expected to be 50 percent white and 50 percent black by early next year.

Crime, though, is still a huge problem.

"The crime statistics show we have stabilised serious crime, but the fact is that we have not brought it down sharply and that is a problem. We have not been able to make much of an impact on social fabric crimes, like violence against the person.

"The root causes of poverty, joblessness, under-education, a culture of violence, disrespect for the elderly and the ruthlessness of criminals, are not strictly policing issues. We can't provide education or housing and the collapse of values and norms makes it difficult for us."

But Mr Fivaz remains upbeat about the future. His five-year contract expires at the end of January next year and no decision has yet been taken on his plans.

"I will do what is best for the organisation and what is best for the country. If the President makes me a new offer, I will consider it. Maybe he, or I, will decide that the most senior post in the police should be more representative.

"I am 53 and not ready for retirement yet. I'm not going to sit back on my stoep. I'll look around and see what options there are. Maybe I will set up a consultancy as there is a great need for that in Africa."

On the reports that he will go to Northern Ireland to take over as chief of the Royal Ulster Constabulary, Mr Fivaz says: "Nobody has approached me. The Patten committee were in South Africa recently and they were very positive about our system and about our transformation process. They thought what we had done here was a workable scenario in their country. But I have not been approached and have not decided on the future so anything more than that is just speculation."

(Fivaz did not move to Northern Ireland, but did establish his own consultancy business after he left the SA Police in 1999)

57 ANDREW FEINSTEIN: 'JUST MORE LIES AND BULLSHIT'

April 6 2000

History, like the smell of canteen lamb curry, collects and lingers in small pockets in the labyrinthine corridors and chambers of the national parliament.

Virtually every nook and cranny has been witness, over the years, to some or other event of import, some whispered deal or betrayal, some whiff of inspiration, some epiphany, some disaster.

Committee Room E249 is no different. It was here, in this well-appointed, comfortably air-conditioned venue just above the National Assembly chamber, that the apartheid era House of Delegates used to meet at the time when PW Botha was State President in the 1980s.

That set a precedent, of sorts. From the start, according to one parliamentary veteran, more "lies and bullshit" were spoken in E249 than in any other room of the century old complex.

It is a proud tradition that continues today.

E249 these days is the home turf to the standing committee on public accounts, or Scopa, if you're on the mailing list.

Scopa is a terrifying institution for the large majority of civil servants. Its central function, after all, is to make sure that government departments make proper and efficient use of taxpayers' money.

Instinctively, one would say there is no correlation at between these two notions. Like military intelligence, efficient government spending is a contradiction in terms.

What is worse for our grey technocrats is that the members of Scopa are unrestrained by party loyalty - and cross the floor to consult and chat with scarcely a thought - and that they believe their responsibilities with a determination bordering on obsession.

Listen to the words of Andrew Feinstein, the ANC MP who was given the chair temporarily this week: "Public money is just that. It is not the government's money, the booty of elected representatives or the money of officials. It is the money of each and every citizen. The less than optimal use of that money - through ill intent, inefficiency or inappropriate or inadequate financial management systems - is a betrayal of all South Africans ... We, on behalf of Parliament, are the guardians of this money and see any less than optimal use thereof in most serious light."

Scarcely a nobler word has ever been uttered in Parliament. One almost expected the false skylight above E249 to come crashing down or the fake marble tiles to part like the Red Sea.

Fortunately, equilibrium and the demands of decades of tradition were quickly restored.

It was only moments before lies and bullshit once more graced the microphones of E249. For the occasion this week was the appearance of the department of welfare whose highest officials were expected to explain the chaotic state of the department's financial management systems and its abject failure to pass millions of rands on to the poor.

Now we all know that to err is to be human. Human nature has contrived a variety of options. They include: lie, deny, obfuscate, blame someone else, apologise, promise to do better, or a combination of the above. There's also the notion of taking responsibility, but we're talking real world options here.

In the hot seat in E249 on Wednesday as the new director general of the welfare department, Angela Bester. Her predicament was explaining why her department, according to the Auditor General, had used less than one percent of the R203-million it received for poverty relief in the 1998/99 financial year and why R353-million, or 78.5 percent of the department's total allocated funds went unspent over the same period.

This was an unenviable task, especially for someone who had been at the department for only a few months.

Her main strategy of defence, though she used almost all of them, was option 3: obfuscate. In this area, those steeped in the strange language of the welfare sector have always enjoyed a special advantage.

I provide here a few classic examples of welfare babble along with their assumed meaning: "It's all variable and depends on a system of cluster co-ordinators" (I have no idea how much it's going to cost or even who to ask); "It is important to understand the context of how the department is operating" (I have no idea how it got this bad); "There is some discontinuity in the work of the department (Nothing is being done); "Many multi-projects are developmental and experimental in nature" (I have no idea what we are supposed to be doing); "There is increasingly an inter-departmental integrated approach to implementation in which consultation means lead times are expanded" (We're late); "We want to sharpen up on the targeting of poverty pockets" (Where did you say the poor people live?).

The committee, of course, could hardly believe their ears. But it was more incredulity than anger.

"I just feel we are going around in circles and are getting lost in a whirlwind of information that doesn't make any sense," lamented Mr Feinstein.

In the end, though, everybody present knew exactly what the problem entailed, in spite of the attempt at obfuscation.

The truth, simply, is that the department of welfare is chaotically managed, missing dozens of senior financial officers, low on morale, under-equipped, poorly trained, unrepresentative, inadequately monitored and is squandering millions in taxpayers' money with no clue how to stop it.

The only consolation is that we at least have a committee in place that is able to peer through the veil of obfuscation and which now has the power to force change even in the welfare department. It's not much, but it's a start.

58 MORGAN TSVANGIRAI: MAN IN THE SHADOWS

April 14 2000

These are busy times for Morgan Tsvangirai, the man who believes he is so close to taking Robert Mugabe's presidency he can almost taste it.

Tsvangirai is the 48-year-old leader of Zimbabwe's only credible opposition party, the Movement for Democratic Change (MDC). And "movement" is exactly what it was this week as he and a coterie of his top officials went on a whistle-stop tour of South Africa and then on to London to raise funds, boost his profile and bolster his hopes for high office.

Elections in Zimbabwe are scheduled for little more than four months hence, so hardly a moment can be wasted if 25 years of ZANU-PF rule are to be ended.

Above the distant roar of jet engines and the nearby crinkling of Bakers biscuit packets, Tsvangirai addressed a makeshift news conference at Cape Town International airport on Wednesday evening.

The immediate impression was of a man in a great hurry.

"Our time is very tight," an aide said, even as he was ushered into the VIP lounge. Destiny, it seems, waits for no one.

The second impression was that he won't be winning any prizes for dress sense, outfitted as he was in a Harris Tweed jacket, a clashing check tie and a purple shirt. Then again, pre-liberation chic in South Africa was hardly cutting-edge fashion. Even now, looking around at what some of our own politicians wore at the Opening of Parliament ceremony, Tsvangirai is not entirely out of kilter with local standards of poor taste.

Perhaps a new suit for his acceptance speech would be a good idea.

But we were not there to judge him on his tie selection. Nor was it his fault that a bout of 'flu, exacerbated by air travel, had rendered his voice gruff and strained.

We went to hear what a person who could be the next president of Zimbabwe had to say about the political and economic crisis that is gripping his country, about the incumbent president and about what policies we might expect from a victorious MDC.

He certainly "talked the talk". His words were littered with references to democracy, change, accountability, transparency, reform, respect for the rule of law, equity, and the whole lexicon of PC nomenclatura that can only have impressed potential donors and supporters.

The general gist is that he would pull Zimbabwean troops out of the Congo, stamp out corruption, introduce economic reforms and speed up the democratic process.

Other than troop withdrawal, which he confessed he would take "some time", the bulk of his responses sounded a bit hollow, a little rehearsed and more general and platitudinous than would prove useful after an electoral victory.

Listen to his response to what he would do with Zimbabwe's economy after an MDC victory: "We require some short-term measures to stabilise the economy and to alleviate the business, foreign exchange, and debt crises. It would be necessary for the government to deal with that in a most pragmatic way. A debt rescheduling programme needs to be put in place. Corruption that is bleeding the economy to alarming proportions needs to be addressed. Government itself must be right-sized. We can't afford 52 ministers of cabinet rank. A clear recovery programme must be started in which the prioritisation of business must be emphasised and in which more investment is put into social sectors such as housing, education and health."

These are good words, but they are far short of a concrete plan.

Likewise, when asked specifically about how he would resolve the land question in Zimbabwe, his comments were generally vague, often repetitive and specifically obvious.

"Zimbabwe is facing a crisis today that has been caused by the leadership failing to implement fundamental land reform," he huffed. "Instead they have put the emphasis on Britain when we have been a sovereign state for the last 25 years. You must accept that land reform is part of the economic reform that is needed in Zimbabwe. It is something every Zimbabwean feels strongly about. Everyone agrees that land reform must be undertaken. But we do need a sound, equitable and transparent process. There must be an observance of the rule of law. People cannot be allowed to run about like outlaws and bandits."

Once again, the bit about the law and the bandits was excellent and no doubt will be well received. But where is the draft policy? The blueprint? How do we know things would be different under a Tsvangirai administration?

Zimbabweans are in trouble to a certain degree because an oppressive political system has prevented the emergence of any other credible leaders within government or the opposition.

Mr Tsvangirai, at this stage, would appear to be all there is to offer. And while this may be a distinct improvement on the current state of affairs, he is hardly a man of charisma punting a revolutionary vision of democracy.

Still he, at least, is making the effort. He is travelling the world spreading his name, raising funds and preaching change.

If he is all Zimbabwe has got, then he will have to do. He may well be advised, though, to sit down at some stage over the next four months and add some substance to his policies. At least then Zimbabweans will know for what and for whom they are voting.

59 JACOB ZUMA FACES QUESTION TIME

May 18 2000

Jacob Zuma, leader of government business and deputy president, laughs comfortably on the front bench of the National Assembly. The gold frames of his glasses glint in the artificial light. His bald head shines.

Standing by his side, Smangaliso Mkhatshwa, deputy minister of education, has either told an exceptionally amusing joke or is just witness to the enduring, unflappable good humour of one of South Africa's most senior politicians.

As deputy president, Zuma stands first in line to inherit the country's highest post, though this will likely only be in 2009. But it is worth observing the man in the meantime, for our fortunes may yet depend on his dapper shoulders.

I won't go into Zuma's political credentials as they are long and impressive. He has certainly served his time and risen through the ranks. I especially enjoy the story of his clandestine journey to Switzerland in the late 1980s at the side of Thabo Mbeki to meet with South African intelligence agents. The meeting was the first between the exiled ANC and official representatives of the apartheid state.

But that is all ancient history now. This week, clad in an elegant azure suit - eclipsed only by the consistently fashionable minister of defence Mosiuoa Lekota - Zuma prepared to face the National Assembly for Question Time.

Now much has changed even in the last year with the way in which Question Time works. In Britain, the Prime Minister is forced to answer questions off the cuff twice a week. This is deemed an important part of democracy.

In South Africa, until recently, the president was also made to face the music on a regular basis.

The powers that be, in their wisdom, have decided however that the president will only answer questions in Parliament once a quarter. It has also decided that political parties will get to ask questions in a certain order and proportionally to their presence in the National Assembly.

Thus, the ANC, which only got to ask one or two laughably sycophantic questions a week now gets to ask most of the questions. And the Democratic Party, which gave government a good, regular grilling on matters of policy, has been relegated to a peripheral role.

The reorganisation of Question Time in Parliament is scandalous. The disbursement of propagandistic puffery should be left to the Government Communication and Information Service and, some would argue, the South African Broadcasting Corporation and not be allowed to undermine an important mechanism of accountability and good governance.

Still, that's not Zuma's problem. All that is required of him is to enjoy the distinctly unchallenging new format. Once the House has been brought to order, the first question is, of course, from the ANC. It's a real tester penned by Mr Mewa Ramgobin: What was South Africa's involvement in the African-European Union summit in Cairo? What progress has been made in respect of a strategic partnership between Europe and Africa and what specified benefits will result from the summit for the African continent?

Grateful for the anticipated set-up, Zuma begins reading uninterestingly from his prepared verbatim response: "Blah blah, crucial role, blah, blah, considerable progress, blah, blah, new partnership, blah blah."

Ramgobin, newly enlightened, added some other perfunctory remark which

Zuma accepted like a compliment, and then sat down.

The DP's first chance came with a follow-up question from one of the party's newest talents, Raenette Taljaard. But Taljaard, perhaps through inexperience, asked about 12 sub-questions one after the other, and Zuma was able to evade them all comfortably by answering none.

Boy Geldenhuys, by contrast one of the longest-serving members in Parliament, focused on one issue only, that of debt relief: what was government's position and what conditions applied? The New National Party foreign affairs spokesperson asked.

Again, no problem for Zuma, though. "South Africa's position is well known. We are calling for debt to be cancelled, with no conditions."

A little later, Kenneth Meshoe from the excruciatingly conservative African Christian Democratic Party asked Zuma whether, like Uganda, South Africa was considering promoting a campaign of abstinence to fight HIV-Aids.

Zuma chuckled again at this bizarre query. "Yes, we are aware of the campaign that encourages people to abstain from..." and here he hesitated for just a moment, "wrong things". It was an odd choice of words and was strangely self-conscious given the porcelain red ribbon lapel badge which Zuma was wearing and which is de rigeur in Tuynhuys these days.

Perhaps the most revealing moment of the afternoon came toward the end when Zuma responded to a NNP question on government's seeming inability to implement laws that had already been passed by Parliament.

Zuma, as leader of government business, should have known that the list of these bills is as long as the ANC's schedule of friendly questions to ministers. From tobacco regulations and use of force by police in arrests to protection of the elderly and security of tenure, they are as numerous as they are important.

As far as he knew, Zuma said, there was only one such law. He then went on to admit that he was "working out a mechanism to deal with the implementation of laws".

The obvious contradiction was baffling but probably pointed at an understandable reluctance to admit in public the government's difficulties in implementing its legislative programme.

As for Zuma? Well, he was comfortable enough in the limelight, quite adept at ducking questions, not shy of a good waffle but still vulnerable to the challenges of the truth. We will watch his progress with interest.

60 KGALEMA MOTLANTHE: WHY THE ANC YOUTH LEAGUE IS FAILING

14 July 2000

I am beginning to think that it is a peculiar South African trait that we all seem to do far better as underdogs than as the overwhelming favourites. Put us with our backs against the wall with only the faintest glimmer of hope and, more often than not, we will prevail. Give us a headstart and the cast-iron certainty of success and we tend to get distracted, lazy, over-elaborate and, quite frequently, beaten.

The African National Congress faced a dilemma of a similar kind as it met to gaze at its collective navel in Port Elizabeth this week.

Stripped of the nobility of the struggle and with little opposition to speak of, it has begun to realise that organisational inertia, individual self-interest and infighting are often the bedfellows of unchallenged, undirected power.

Every day, the struggle era recedes and with it the urgency of those days. What does the new generation have to inspire it now? The dragon is dead, and St George must learn to dance.

The ANC no longer has a monster to tilt at, and the past grows less of an excuse with each year it governs.

The ANC's greatest enemy now, ironically, is normality. When things are normal, it is difficult to excite people. The youth, freed from the burdens of actual revolution, re-engage the virtual one against their parents, social expectations, and each other.

A good barometer of the state of a political organisation can be found in its youth structures. In the late 1940s and 1950s, the growing radicalism of the ANC's Youth League forced head-to-head confrontation with initially the party and then the state.

Now, six years after the party's accession to power, the Youth League is dissipating.

According to a report presented this week by secretary general Kgalema Motlanthe, young activists have been opting for the ANC itself rather than the Youth League.

This was causing the league to suffer weak and collapsed branches and resources were drying up, Motlanthe noted.

This is not a good sign for any political party and Motlanthe is right to be alarmed. This is particularly given the fact that he himself must be held responsible for what has obviously been a rapid degeneration in party structures.

As secretary general, it is his job and mission to bolster and grow the organisation. He is patently not achieving these objectives.

"The challenge currently facing us is how to interest the youth in the process of social change," Motlanthe told the ANC.

But other unnerving things are happening within the majority party.

The branches themselves are wavering. Discussions in the branches focus more these days, says the report, on "personal differences and conflicts" than on key policy issues.

Such an outcome is not a total surprise in an organisation which treats lack of discipline as a cardinal sin and thereby diminishes anyone's willingness to stand up and be critical.

If the ANC's alliance partners, the South African Communist Party and the Congress of South African Trade Unions, cannot stand up to the majority party and win, what chance do individuals have within it?

Both alliance partners have been emasculated by the ANC's commitment to its economic objectives (as contained in the Growth, Employment and Redistribution Strategy) as well as to its programme to privatise state assets. The consequence has been an incredibly solid and internationally hailed economy and deep frustration among the minor alliance partners.

Disagreement with party policy either has to be tolerated or, as with the recent case of ANC media liaison officer Peter Venter, conducted with symbolic handing over of your membership card.

President Thabo Mbeki, in his opening address to the conference on Wednesday, again raised the problem of "careerists" within the ANC.

"We ... continue to retain opportunists and careerists in our ranks ... they join the sole aim of furthering their personal careers and using the access to state power we have as a ruling to enrich themselves."

Frankly, I think it is a bit naive to expect young, intelligent people to join an organisation, even a political one, for purely altruistic reasons. Of course they have a career in mind. Of course they will leap at opportunities to move into leadership positions.

The problem is not so much the ambition of youth but the ethical codes and practices of the party itself. Mbeki frequently talks about how, when he and his peers were young, they never thought for a moment about joining the ANC to further their careers.

But these are different times. Normal times. Kids get into politics because they enjoy the tussle of different views, because they believe in the underlying values of the party, because they respect the leadership and because there might be a future in it for them. There's nothing wrong with that.

A critical element of the ANC's difficulties at present is one of leadership. It is apparent that Motlanthe is not doing a good enough job. The problems of careerists, failing branches, dwindling memberships and a flat youth league are not being raised in Port Elizabeth for the first time. They were raised at Mafikeng for the last congress and before that in Bloemfontein.

There has been no palpable evidence of any genuine strategy which attempts to tackle these issues, only repeated warnings of what are now comfortably established phenomena.

Finally, Mbeki has won praise from a number of corners for his rallying call of an African renaissance.

It would appear, however, that this vision is failing to inspire either the grassroots membership or the civil service. This may be because the message of the vision is getting caught up on the way by inefficient and impermeable structures.

But it could also mean that the vision has no resonance for ordinary people. Instead of being the glue that holds the party together, it is the tightly wrapped fist through which the sand will inevitably slip.

61 IN DESMOND TUTU'S HONOUR

July 9 2000

More than ten years ago, a small group of staffers working under Archbishop Desmond Tutu wondered what they could do to celebrate the Nobel Peace Prize laureate's life and spirit. The recent public launch of plans for the Desmond Tutu Peace Centre was the realisation of their dream.

In the mid-1980s, a young Anglican priest, Chris Ahrends, was doing what he could to minister to a deeply traumatised community near Swellendam in the Boland.

The town, called Ashton, was at war with itself. On one side, the fiery youth sounded the drum of liberation. On the other, the conservative, frustrated older generation, the "witdoeke", brutalised their own young to preserve a way of life.

Stirring up the pot was the Swellendam Security Police. Attempting to calm it down were the church workers. It was a pattern of misery and pain being repeated in countless small towns from one end of apartheid South Africa to the other.

In the midst of the turmoil, Ahrends received a summons from Bishopscourt in Cape Town, the Church of the Province of South Africa's seat of power. The newly appointed and already highly controversial Archbishop, Desmond Mpilo Tutu, required the young priest's attendance.

Ahrends still doesn't know why it was that he was called to become Tutu's chaplain. But, like many who have come into contact with the Nobel Peace Prize laureate over the years, his life was to be changed by the experience.

From the start, the work was gruelling. Tutu was up at 5am and had a strict regime of prayer, meetings and engagements that often went deep into the night. Ahrends's tasks were varied and demanding. In the days, he tried to ensure Tutu was given time for worship, rest and meditation. In the evening, he drove Tutu to his engagements and made sure he got home safely.

Tutu kept a file with all the people he needed to pray for in it. "Every single day he prayed for each and every cabinet member by name. He prayed for those in prison and those in exile, he prayed for this priest's child and that person in trouble. His prayers criss-crossed the globe like a travel book," laughs Arends.

"It's a file this thick," he says, a good four inches between his stretched thumb and middle finger.

"The Arch used to say that my job was never over until I'd put a glass of sherry in his hand last thing at night," says Ahrends. "In fact, he preferred a rum and coke".

Ask anyone who has spent time with Tutu what they find endearing, impressive or inspiring about the man and they will give you a range of different reasons.

For Ahrends, it was his ability to empathise, his "cavernous mind for information", his extraordinary wisdom and intelligence and his sense of humour.

"He had a great capacity for joke telling. I don't know where a sense of humour comes from but I think that when you are so in touch with your own humanity, you laugh a lot and you cry a lot. We laughed and laughed and laughed even though those were very tense and traumatic times.

"He is a remarkable man. So human, so vulnerable, so needy".

These are sentiments common enough amongst those who have got to know

Tutu. "A number of us were caught up in his episcopacy," says Ahrends. With Tutu's laughter and his spirit, he evoked a passionate sense of loyalty among his friends as well as a fervent belief that his was a life to be cherished and celebrated.

Back in the mid to late 1980s, a small circle of Tutu's former staff - including Colin Jones, the first black Dean of St George's Cathedral - were already talking about finding a way to capture Tutu's spirit for future generations.

"The idea for some kind of centre was talked about in 1988/89 but the Arch said he didn't want anything named after him until he retired."

When he retired, Tutu then moved the goalposts and said he didn't want to proceed with the idea until he had finished with the Truth and Reconciliation Commission (TRC), of which he was the chairperson.

"At the end of the TRC process, I told him we wanted to come and give him a presentation. We sat him down and told him about our idea," says Ahrends.

At root, the idea of the Desmond Tutu Peace Centre was the notion of hope.

"We wanted to honour Tutu's capacity to point to the future. His only real mission was to explain that we are all one family, and we must not forget that. No one is in exile in God's family because we all belong in it together. It was a naive dream made profound by a man like Tutu. It also goes to the spirit of our renaissance, of where Africa is going, of being one family in Africa."

In October 1998, Tutu agreed with the small group that they should proceed with their plan. A legal entity, the Desmond Tutu Peace Trust, was created and a German non-governmental organisation, Bread of the World, donated R50,000 to get the team going.

More funds came in from the Evangelical Missionary Society and eight trustees from a diversity of religions and backgrounds were appointed to oversee the project. Ahrends was appointed director.

Now, some 20 months later, the Desmond Tutu Peace Centre project has developed into an extraordinarily ambitious plan combining interactive tourist attraction, world class study and research institution and business venture all rolled into one.

The recent announcement that Coca Cola would invest $1-million in the project has rocketed the idea from fancy into fact.

The trustees are currently looking for a suitable site in Cape Town of at least four hectares and an international design competition is soon to be launched. It is envisaged the centre will cover about 6,500 square metres and will have a "cool zone" especially aimed at the young.

The centre is also expected to include a library as well as a leadership academy.

The academy will not focus on the traditional "business school-type skills", says the director of the Desmond Tutu Leadership Academy, Glenda Wildschut, but on "soft skills" like self-awareness and personal growth.

"We want to be able to produce an African-based understanding of what leadership is about," says Wildschut. "We also want to work on the notion of peace and what it means and not work for the cessation of war which is a different thing."

Like the centre, the leadership academy also boasts an ambitious vision. It includes existing and future leaders co-operating and interacting together, a focus on the moral and ethical requirements and demands of contemporary leadership, a women's leadership programme and the creation of a Chair in Leadership and Future Studies based at three African universities.

A vital element to the plan, however, is the absolute necessity to make the project commercially viable and sustainable, says Ahrends.

"You don't want to put up a white elephant in the name of Tutu. It must work."

For the moment, though, many of the plans have a dream-like quality. The small team is still holed up in the crumbling surroundings of the Old Granary, one of Cape Town's most ancient structures. There are holes in the wall and the windows are bare. The bulk of the promised donations and cash hasn't quite arrived yet.

But if there's one thing the founders of the Desmond Tutu Peace Centre have in abundance, it's hope. And hope, as Tutu himself would agree, will take you a long way toward a dream.

62 SOUTH AFRICA'S MIRACLE: HOW DID YOU DO THAT?

September 1 2000

More than a few people will groan at the prospect of digesting the details and implications of this week's National Conference on Racism.

Why on earth would anyone be interested in another government talk shop which, like similar exercises on poverty and HIV/Aids, seems incapable of doing anything genuinely constructive or useful?

We all know racism exists in South Africa. How can it not after 300 years of colonialism and 50 years of apartheid?

One argument for why such an examination of the national navel is a useful and indeed essential mission is that we simply owe it to the world to explain how we did it.

We are, after all, the rainbow nation, the scene of the miracle. Somehow, we managed to avert a civil war and emerge triumphant.

Even the Truth and Reconciliation Commission is heralded internationally as a pathbreaking initiative to nurture national unity in the face of almost overwhelming historical conditions.

But it may also be the case, as President Thabo Mbeki argued in his speech opening the conference earlier this week, that "unfortunately we have not done the necessary work to assess what it was that made it possible for the miracle to happen, being seemingly content merely to bask in the universal praise."

In other words: how did we do it? Has anyone really thought for a moment about how we managed to pull it off six years ago? Was it just our leaders doing what they should be doing? Was it something located deep inside the South African psyche or was it just blind luck?

Perhaps we should know?

Mbeki also pointed out that no other country in the world has succeeded in creating a truly non-racial society.

"Many across the globe believe, with good reason, that because of our specific history, we have the possibility and will make an important contribution to the universal struggle to defeat the scourge of racism ... our government is convinced that, as a people, we have the capacity to achieve this historic and epoch-making objective.

"We are convinced that as a people, both black and white, we have the wisdom, ingenuity and sensitivity to the human condition that will drive and enable us to overcome the demon of racism".

These are extraordinary claims. Are they figments of fantasy or does Mandela's heir have a point?

This, you will agree, is a slightly different way of looking at race. Suddenly, it is not a casting around for who will take the blame and who will say they are sorry loudest. It is the acknowledgement that, like the antidote to poison, South Africans somehow stumbled on a solution to racism from within racism itself.

But perhaps it is overly optimistic to expect something so revolutionary as a solution to centuries of racism to come bounding out of the conference centre in Sandton this week.

Some will argue that the creation of an Other is an inevitable obsession of the human condition. It is as natural as greed and envy. If it is not race, it will be something else, like height or weight, that separates us from each other.

If we are lucky enough to discover the magical antidote to racism, boosting it within our own society and replicating it in others is the next logical step.

We need to know how to confront and overcome racism.

This will be the second important task of the conference this week: to come up with practical, feasible methods of combatting racism.

The chances are that like poverty and HIV/Aids, the solution to racism lies in addressing the complex social inequities lying at the root of modern society. In addition, it is a matter of attitude and behaviour.

As Mbeki pointed out in his speech, the first steps toward overcoming racism in South Africa have already been taken. First, we have evaded the worst case scenario: the possibility of all-out race war. Second, we have put in place a constitutional and legal framework that forbids prejudice on many grounds, including race.

Quite what the next step should be is open to question. Aside from identifying what it is in the national psyche that militates against racism, more material prospects need to be considered.

How, for instance, do we de-racialise our living arrangements? Spatially we are overwhelmingly tied into the apartheid planners' grand vision of racial separatedness. That is no way to overcome racism. We have to live together, that is a given.

We also have to go to school together, play sport together and, piece by piece, break down the deeply ingrained and resilient barriers of prejudice.

There is so much more, from the creation of role models to the celebration of an individual's or a community's special talents.

The simple message is that considering issues of race need not mean the imminent occurence of bad or negative things. It doesn't have to be about finger-pointing or about apologies about guilt or een about entitlement.

It should also be about learning what we did right and finding a way of doing it again. It should be about showing the world that the miracle is possible elsewhere too. And it should be about creating a future in which race plays a diminishing role in characterising the inhabitants and accomplishments of this rainbow nation.

63 THABO MBEKI: THE CHIEF

December 20 2000

With an AIDS badge on his lapel and an ostrich leather folder under his arm, President Thabo Mbeki rose to face the music in Parliament yesterday.

MPs don't often get a chance to take on 'the chief' these days. He's either overseas or they're on recess. When the opportunity does come round, once every three months for the official President's Question Time, they like to make the most of it.

South Africa's policy on Zimbabwe and land invasions, racism, marginalisation, a secret conspiracy to topple the presidency (denied) and last, but by no means least, the vexing issue of HIV and Aids were all ranked as the matters most MPs wanted to hear about from the president.

An hour hardly seemed adequate for such hefty matters, but the representatives of the people wanted to know and had the opportunity to ask.

It would be some time before Mbeki was allowed to get into the answers, though.

For twenty minutes, Mbeki did little more than stand by the podium listening to a minor row over procedure.

Opposition parties were incensed by a late move to combine parts of questions so that each query concerned a single topic.

"The rules of the House are simply being disregarded," protested the Democratic Party's Chief Whip Douglas Gibson.

After a while, Mbeki intervened.

His points were punctuated with both hands on the podium, as if he was playing slow chords on a piano.

He appeared to convince most present that the suggested changes were made in good faith and the rest accepted the need to get on with proceedings.

His attitude to the looming ordeal was to be his usual strategy: patient, unflappable reasonableness.

The issue of racism, while undoubtedly important, was never really grappled with by the president or his interlocutors. Mbeki praised General Constand Viljoen for his efforts to avert civil war in 1994 and Viljoen, after a round of grateful applause, returned the compliment.

PAC leader Stanley Mogoba urged his colleagues "not to concentrate on colour but concentrate on the land". No-one knew what this meant so they smiled and hoped he would sit down, which he did.

Mbeki was full of conciliatory noises and even-handedness. He rebuked one of his own party for rounding a little too fully on the white community.

"All of us have the obligation to fight racism, whether black or white," he chided. After an even less challenging discussion of Zimbabwe, it was time for the big one: HIV/Aids.

"Does HIV cause Aids?" Mbeki asked out aloud twice, showing the question at least held no fears. It was the answer that was going to prove slightly more problematic.

There are three things you need to know about Mbeki's attitude to HIV and

Aids, each re-emphasised in the National Assembly yesterday.

The first - and probably most important - is that since 1994, government policy surrounding HV/Aids has been premised on the fundamental understanding that the HI Virus causes Aids. This attitude was again reiterated recently following a policy review and will continue to be the country's official position and the anchor of its strategies. On the related subject of condoms and safe sex, government policy is iron-clad in favour of both: "There is absolutely no confusion on this matter," Mbeki said.

The second point is that Mbeki admits partial responsibility for causing confusion on the issue of causality. This was a fairly big step. It could possibly even be the first time that Mbeki has admitted to an error of judgement in the first year and a bit of his administration.

Not that the apology was unqualified. "Perhaps all of us, the way we handled this, may have resulted in that confusion," was how he phrased it.

The third point is that Mbeki is a dissident when it comes to theories of HIV and its link to Aids. He cannot accept the hypothesis that HIV alone causes the collapse of the immune system defined as the syndrome that is Aids.

Pressed to inject himself with a cc of Aids-infected blood to prove his scepticism, the President declined. Pushed to at least test himself for HIV, he again deferred.

"People are at liberty to decide whether to check their state of health, or not," he responded to PAC MP Patricia de Lille. "I operate under certain obligations, and I have very regular medical check-ups - and I'm sure it would quite wise for you also to do so."

64 PETER HAIN: A NIGHT ON THE TOWN WITH A MINISTER OF THE CROWN

January 11 2001.

In a painted blue shack in Khayelitsha, a British minister of the crown leans over a pool table with the green ball in his sights.

We are in a shebeen called the Waterfront, aptly and ironically named by Khayelitsha residents who remember when the building housed the only water tap in the area servicing close to 3000 homes.

It is a key moment in the game. The crowd hushes. The minister's opponent, a little ashamed at his own success thus far, shuffles from one foot to the other.

The green ball is about three inches from the corner pocket, glinting in glorious, vulnerable isolation. Under normal circumstances, it would be a sure thing. Almost.

Peter Hain, the British Foreign Minister, had played enough pool over the years to be confident with the shot. No self-respecting anti-apartheid activist failed to pick up at least a proficiency in bar activities and games.

But these were far from normal circumstances. A good few years had passed by since he had played much. It was also a bit of a distraction to have an audience of two television cameras, a half dozen whirring cameras with motor-drives, a room crowded with reporters, diplomats, a few bemused locals, and a nearby street teeming with excited, noisy children.

Also, he hadn't sunk any balls yet. It was beginning to get embarrassing.

Hain hesitated. He was suffering from what they call 'the yips' in professional sport: a sudden, irrational inability to complete the easy, short shots.

Hain had the yips. The crowd muttered. The media's pens were poised. Hain's reputation as a cool man of the people was on the line.

As the pool cue wavered, a suited aide walked and pointed carefully and helpfully at one side of the ball. A spin doctor perhaps? "Hit it here, sire" he may have said, though no words were used. Hain nodded. The crowd held its breath. The aide stood back.

Hain pulled back the cue and punched the shot. Missed. A great sigh of disappointment filled the darkened room.

"I deliberately didn't pot the balls," a wounded (though smiling) Hain later told guests at a dinner function at Gugu Le Afrika. "I didn't want to show (the locals) up".

After confessing that "actually, I'm out of practice" - and insisting he had eventually sunk "at least two balls" - he spoke eloquently of his optimism about the potential for tourism in South Africa in general and in Khayelitsha in particular.

There is little orthodox or stuffy about Hain. He is certainly the first minister of the British crown to hang out at a shebeen, drink beer and play pool in Khayelitsha, even if it was more a photo opportunity than a heart-to-heart with the residents.

His decision to stay the night at the Kopanong bed and breakfast was also laudatory - though it's unlikely the Cape Grace Hotel or the Mount Nelson will be shaking in their boots just yet.

"If even a British minister can have fun in Khayelitsha, anyone can," he announced later.

It is remarkable to come across so senior a foreign politician with such optimism and confidence about South Africa, even if we know he was born and brought up here.

He is often in the country, has a house in Cape Town and never fails to take the opportunity to do what he can to give South Africa a push in the right direction.

In a statement issued by the British High Commission during the visit, Hain said the Blair administration saw "Thabo Mbeki's government as a dynamic and creative force both in Africa and on global issues from combating weapons to securing debt relief for the poorest countries.

"My message is that South Africa is a great place to invest in, to do business in, to live in and to visit as a tourist." And a grand message it is too. If only all South Africans were similarly convinced, Hain's task would be made considerably easier.

The spotlight put on Khayelitsha by Hain, if a touch contrived, was a worthwhile exercise. The restaurant which hosted him for dinner was a simple venue in a converted, concrete-floored garage. The owner, Abe Bokwe, was the head chef at Blues in Camps Bay before fulfilling a long-held dream to service his own community.

Across from the Site C Waterfront was Vicky's Bed and Breakfast, the home and business of Vicky Ntozini.

The guest house boasts two rooms off a lively street and was established in June last year. Mostly occupied by foreign tourists, it has nevertheless provided a window on authentic township life. Such an experience, perhaps surprisingly to some, is a marketable and valuable asset.

"People must come to see the way I'm living," says Ms Ntozini, a recent finalist in the Entrepreneur of the Year competition, throwing her arms open in welcome.

"They must feel the African vibe and experience the township, the real thing. People don't only want to see the beautiful side of South Africa."

Ms Ntozini and Mr Bokwe are among a growing band of hospitality sector businesspeople establishing themselves in Cape Town's township areas.

Each morning, Ms Ntozini looks at a newspaper advertisement featuring herself outside her bed and breakfast under the headline: "The smallest hotel in South Africa".

"I look at that picture and think, Vicky, you're not only recognised in South Africa but in the whole world".

With her email and website in place, a fetch and drop-off service on offer and the widest smile in Site C, Ms Ntozini is hoping the future holds the promise of the rapid expansion of her business.

"I want a double storey house in a few year's time," she says.

While new tourism-attracting businesses in Khayelitsha, Langa and elsewhere have drawn some attention in the media of late, the focus of international interest brought to bear by Hain is of inestimable value.

Many are tipping Hain to be elevated to Tony Blair's full cabinet.

Frankly, South Africa could hardly hope for a better scenario. Since taking responsibility for Africa, Hain has demonstrated consistent and compassionate understanding and support for South Africa and for the continent as a whole.

It's just the pool skills he's going to have to brush up on if he's really going to make an impact in Khayelitsha.

65 JACOB ZUMA: THE MAN WHO DOESN'T WANT TO BE PRESIDENT

April 6 2001

On Tuesday this week, an extraordinary thing happened.

Deputy President Jacob Zuma issued a formal statement strongly denying rumours of his complicity in an attempted leadership coup aimed at unseating President Thabo Mbeki. The rumoured coup was apparently scheduled for the next party conference in 2002.

In such painted and glossy terms did Zuma paint the presidency, his credentials, his capabilities, his contribution and in such glowing phrases did he depict the unshakeable unity of the ruling party, that anyone reading such a document can only have been immediately suspicious. Could it be that the deputy president, to paraphrase the Bard, "doth protest too much?"

The president was capable, Zuma said. The president had a profound understanding of the movement. The president had shown excellent leadership.

In fact, not only did Zuma declare he had no intention of standing for the position of president, he absolutely had no desire to become president either. This is a strange stance for a deputy president only a heartbeat away from the top job in the land.

We will be sure to remind him of it in years to come. Indeed, it will probably only be a matter of days before Mbeki heads off on his next round of international trips thereby leaving Zuma, as usual, as acting president. What horror this must be for a man of such lukewarm ambition.

What was puzzling was that prior to Zuma's declaration of undying support and love, there had been precious little in the public domain about the rumours that had so horrified the ANC leadership. It was, instead, overwhelmingly an internal crisis with little bearing on the outside world.

At the latest ANC National Executive Meeting, the question of unity was uppermost in many minds. It was agreed that the party could not function as an agent for change if it was divided.

But Zuma, so those close to him say, was so sick and tired of the rumours that he couldn't help himself.

Zuma's own explanation for the rumours sounded positively medieval. There were people from "faceless, destructive quarters", he said, who were determined to "undermine the stability of our organisation".

"We have been aware of some elements in various guises, who have been trying to isolate the President by creating the impression that some of his trusted comrades are plotting against him and, in this way, remove them from him".

Zuma spoke not only of vicious rumours but also of false intelligence reports that besmirched his name and linked him to a secret movement to remove the president.

Now this all seems far-fetched to the casual observer. One would have thought a quiet word in Mbeki's ear and a few firm denials at the NEC would have been sufficient.

But, no, the statement had been issued, said Zuma, "to assure ANC members at all levels, all South Africans and all our international friends, that the ANC remains strong and united and that we will continue to support our leader,

President Mbeki."

Well, we're glad to hear that and find Zuma's panicky denials most reassuring.

To give some context, provincial elections time is looming in the ANC and, thereafter, it's the national conference. Things are hotting up and there's a great deal at stake. A degree of lobbying, back-stabbing, and rumour-mongering is, in any case, hardly the sole preserve of the majority party.

Any political organisation will sympathise with the awkward process of either re-affirming or booting out the leadership.

Frankly, with more than a year to go before the ANC's national conference, the chances of Mbeki getting the chop seem remote at best.

There have been signs of somewhat frigid relations between the president and the deputy president for some time now. The two are said to have clashed over the HIV/Aids debacle, the arms probe and over the reassignment of the rural development programme.

The infrequency of their get-togethers over the first year of the Mbeki presidency became the subject of pithy observation even among the most senior aides.

Things had in any case improved relative to the tension between Mbeki and Nelson Mandela during the last months of the Mandela presidency. One anecdotal tale tells of how Mandela, fed up with being ignore by Mbeki, marched over to his house early one morning and - still wearing his slippers - hammered on Mbeki's kitchen door until he was permitted an audience with his deputy.

Zuma, remember, wasn't even meant to be the deputy president. This job had been cleared for Mangosuthu Buthelezi in an effort to secure KwaZulu-Natal for the ANC and to bind in the Inkatha Freedom Party to a lasting peace. One of the key movers behind this initiative was Zuma.

But now that we know Zuma has ruled himself out of contention for the top job, one begins to ponder who will be Mbeki's heir.

While in all likelihood there are still many years to go before an heir is required, eyes are already being cast around at prospective candidates, whether renegade or serious contender. That, after all, is politics.

Zuma shouldn't worry about that, though, because he's not interested in the presidency. Really, he's not.

(Jacob Zuma took up the post of President of South Africa in 2009)

66 WINNIE MADIKIZELA-MANDELA'S POISONOUS LIPS

June 19 2001

At a rally over the weekend, President Thabo Mbeki brushed off the public attentions of ANC Women's League President Winnie Madikizela-Mandela.

Mbeki has encountered a great deal of flak for giving the so-called Mother of the Nation, Winnie Madikizela-Mandela, the cold shoulder at a rally in Soweto. Frankly, we don't blame him a bit.

Madikizela-Mandela has been a poisonous presence to Mbeki since he took over the reins of power. Already convicted of child abduction, sacked from her deputy ministership and renowned for having one of the weakest attendance records in Parliament, Madikizela-Mandela has set herself up as one of Mbeki's fiercest internal critics.

She has seldom missed an opportunity to berate his government for its failures not to turn celebrated cases of human misfortune to her advantage. Madikizela-Mandela's opportunism was never more evident than at the rally when she arrived an hour late with a huge entourage. Disrupting proceedings and violating protocol, she headed straight for the stage to make a big show of kissing Mbeki.

Unsurprisingly, this was not an especially agreeable prospect for the president.

Here was his arch-critic, the author of a leaked letter which sparked allegations of his womanising, playing the crowd at his expense. It was a slap in the face, and he would have none of it.

Would we have preferred Mbeki to have smiled, waved to the crowd, and acted the picture of pretence and insincerity? There was certainly no physical threat in his action and suggestions to the contrary were more fibs of other opportunities than the facts of what actually happened.

The incident was not a nice sight, but Mbeki was within his rights calmly and pointedly to ward off the looming lips of a woman he palpably cannot stand.

Madikizela-Mandela was no innocent victim, wronged before the world. She is a dishonest manipulator who was simply caught in the act.

67 FRENE GINWALA FACES A STORM

May 25 2001

Few people in South African politics can be as intimidating as the Speaker of the National Assembly, Frene Ginwala.

When she presides over a sitting of her beloved House, she puts up with no nonsense whatever. Her calls of "order, order" reverberate powerfully through the chamber forcing obedience among even the most recalcitrant - or senior - members.

A summons to the Speaker's office is seldom anticipated by MPs with anything other than a feeling of dread.

Since 1994, Ginwala has been at the very helm of South African democracy, guiding Parliament through the choppy waters of the first few months and presiding over the passage of hundreds of nation-changing pieces of legislation.

None would dispute that Parliament in 2001 is a friendlier, more transparent, diverse, credible and more democratic institution than it was only ten years ago.

A considerable proportion of the credit for this is due to Ginwala whose tough exterior, intimate grasp of the rules and hefty intelligence has given the process sorely needed gravitas. Add to this the Speaker's passionate interest in and understanding of South African history and her equally determined sense of national pride, and you have a formidable presence glaring at you over her glasses.

Suddenly, though, the rug has been swept from under Ginwala's feet. Twice she offered to resign this week following allegations that she was in dereliction of her duties and had shown bias in her handling of the arms deal investigation.

In the seven years she has been Speaker, this has been by far the worst.

She has been attacked by the chairman of the public accounts committee, the Inkatha Freedom Party's Gavin Woods, for undermining the committee's oversight role. It was United Democratic Movement leader Bantu Holomisa who accused her in a public letter of dereliction of duty and bias. African Christian Democratic Party leader Kenneth Meshoe and Democratic Alliance leader Tony Leon have both had harsh words to say about Ginwala's performance of late.

This had not been Ginwala's "finest hour" said Leon in a statement during the week: "Where she should have stood up and defended Parliament and its most powerful committee against executive-minding, bullying and cajoling, she seemed to join the other side. I would remind Dr Ginwala that her paramount duty is to advance the interests of the legislature against all comers, including the government".

It seems that South Africa's political system has reached a crossroads of sorts.

Parliament's effectively been too busy over the last seven years dismantling apartheid and creating the legislative building blocks of a new kind of society to worry about too much about esoteric matters like the separation of powers.

Now that "normality" has been achieved in the broad sense, the arms deal investigation has forced a fundamental reassessment of the state of the political system.

A whole series of questions have been thrown up: How accountable should the executive be to Parliament? How much independence should be wielded by oversight bodies like the public accounts committee and the ethics committee?

And, crucially for Ginwala, when should the Speaker be neutral and when should party loyalty determine the Speaker's actions?

The ANC has consistently shown difficulty in differentiating between party and state.

The latest example, which Safety and Security Minister Steve Tshwete failed to disprove this week in spite of a direct question on the issue, is the apparent use of the state's intelligence services to investigate an internal leadership squabble.

The blurring of party and state, which has been evident for some years, was perhaps the first symptom of a growing crisis which has now burst into the open and which has thrown the legislative tier into confusion.

The ship Ginwala has been guiding with such comfort and skill for the last seven years has suddenly hit a fierce Cape storm.

The Constitution, as rushed as it was, provides no help in defining what exactly the role of the Speaker should be. Thus far, it has been a matter of custom. The assumption has been that the Speaker is a determinedly neutral referee, an arbiter of parliamentary rules and disputes, whose overriding function is to ensure and uphold the reputation and prestige of the institution.

But how can she be these things if she is a senior and loyal member of the majority party?

In the Westminster model, the Speaker resigns all party affiliation and responsibilities for the duration of his or her tenure. In the United States, the function is more partisan.

Neither is necessarily right or wrong. But we do have to choose what we want. She cannot be both referee and player. It was in attempting this dual role, allege the opposition, that the current problems have been encountered.

South African politics has reached an intriguing moment. The outcome will not be the collapse of democracy nor will it presage the emergence of tyranny.

But it will have an impact on the quality of our democracy. Specifically, the resolution of the current crisis will determine Parliament's capacity to hold the executive accountable and its ability to function in spite of the strong party system. It will also decide the future role of the Speaker.

Ginwala has done an extraordinary job over the last seven years. Her real legacy, though, will be determined over the next few weeks.

ABOUT THE AUTHOR

Adrian Hadland worked as a political editor and parliamentary correspondent in South Africa for more than ten years covering the extraordinary period between the end of the last white, apartheid "tricameral" government in the early 1990s and the country's third democratic election in 2004. Hailed by the Foreign Correspondents' Association in South Africa for his "outstanding" reportage, Adrian has published more than 20 books including a biography of Nelson Mandela, an unauthorized biography of Thabo Mbeki, the memoirs of Kader Asmal and various academic and policy-oriented works. He is currently Chair of Journalism and Media Studies at the University of Stirling in the UK.

Printed in Great Britain
by Amazon

62641173R00157